DATE DUE

NO 3 - 9			

THE THIRD AMENDMENT

The ★★★★★★ AMERICAN HERITAGE HISTORY *of the* BILL *of* RIGHTS

THE THIRD AMENDMENT

Burnham Holmes

Introduction by

WARREN E. BURGER

Chief Justice of the United States
1969–1986

Silver Burdett Press

For Ken

Cover: U.S. troops. The Third Amendment grew out of the colonists' fear that the British might force private citizens to give room and board to soldiers in their homes.

CONSULTANTS:

Fred Anderson
Professor of History
University of Colorado
Boulder, Colorado

Maria Cedeño
Social Studies District Coordinator
Law-Related Education Coordinator
Dade County Public Schools
Miami, Florida

Text and Cover Design: Circa 86, Inc.

Library of Congress Cataloging-in-Publication Data

Holmes, Burnham.
  The Third Amendment/by Burnham Holmes; with an introduction by
Warren E. Burger.
    p. cm.—(The American Heritage history of the Bill of
Rights)
  Includes bibliographical references (p. 92) and indexes.
  Summary: Studies the historical circumstances in the American colonies that eventually led to the drafting of the Third Amendment, which forbids the arbitrary quartering of troops in private homes.
    1. United States—Constitutional law—Amendments—3rd—History—
Juvenile literature. 2. Requisitions, Military—United States—
History—Juvenile literature. [1. United States—Constitutional
law—Amendments—3rd—History.] I. Title. II. Series.
KF4558 3rd.H65 1991
342.73'03—dc20
[347.3023]

                                                              90-24482
                                                                   CIP
                                                                    AC

Manufactured in the United States of America.

ISBN 0-382-24181-9 [lib. bdg.]
10 9 8 7 6 5 4 3 2 1

ISBN 0-382-24194-0 [pbk.]
10 9 8 7 6 5 4 3 2 1

$\mathscr{C}$ONTENTS

INTRODUCTION

WARREN E. BURGER
Chief Justice of the United States, 1969–1986

The Third Amendment may be thought obsolete in protecting private citizens from being forced to provide housing for soldiers. It is a very specific liberty, but an important one to Americans of the Framers' generation. But its concept of individual freedom and liberty is much broader than that.

Concepts of liberty—the values liberty protects—inspired the Framers of our Constitution and the Bill of Rights to some of their most impassioned eloquence. "Liberty, the greatest of earthly possessions— give us that precious jewel, and you may take everything else," declaimed Patrick Henry. Those toilers in the "vineyard of liberty" sensed the historic nature of their mission, and their foresight accounts for the survival of the Bill of Rights.

The philosophy embodied in the Third Amendment is derived from the American colonists' fear of British military power. Though that danger is long past, the Third Amendment still embodies the same basic principles: that the military must be subject to civilian control, and that the government cannot intrude into private homes without good reason.

The long-term success of the system of ordered liberty set up by our Constitution was by no means foreordained. The bicentennial of the Bill of Rights provides an opportunity to reflect on the significance of the freedoms we enjoy and to commit ourselves to exercise the civic responsibilities required to sustain our constitutional system. The Constitution, including its first ten amendments, the Bill of Rights, has survived two centuries because of its unprecedented philosophical premise: that it derives its power from the people. It is not a grant from the government to the people. In 1787 the masters—the people—were saying to their government—their servant—that certain rights are inherent, natural rights and that they belong to the people, who had those rights before any governments existed. The function of government, they said, was to protect these rights.

The Bill of Rights also owes its continued vitality to the fact that it was drafted by experienced, practical politicians. It was a product of the Framers' essential mistrust of the frailties of human nature. This led them to develop the idea of the separation of powers and to make the Bill of Rights part of the permanent Constitution.

Moreover, the document was designed to be flexible, and the role of providing that flexibility through interpretation has fallen to the judiciary. Indeed, the first commander in chief, George Washington, gave the Supreme Court its moral marching orders two centuries ago when he said, "the administration of justice is the firmest pillar of government." The principle of judicial review as a check on government has perhaps nowhere been more significant than in the protection of individual liberties. It has been my privilege, along with my colleagues on the Court, to ensure the continued vitality of our Bill of Rights. As John Marshall asked, long before he became chief justice, "To what quarter will you look for a protection from an infringement on the Constitution, if you will not give the power to the judiciary?"

But the preservation of the Bill of Rights is not the sole responsibility of the judiciary. Rather, judges, legislatures, and presidents are partners with every American; liberty is the responsibility of every public officer and every citizen. In this spirit all Americans should become acquainted with the principles and history of this most remarkable document. Its bicentennial should not be simply a celebration but the beginning of an ongoing process. Americans must—by their conduct—guarantee that it continues to protect the sacred rights of our uniquely multicultural population. We must not fail to exercise our rights to vote, to participate in government and community activities, and to implement the principles of liberty, tolerance, opportunity, and justice for all.

THE AMERICAN HERITAGE
HISTORY OF THE BILL OF RIGHTS

THE FIRST AMENDMENT
by Philip A. Klinkner

THE SECOND AMENDMENT
by Joan C. Hawxhurst

THE THIRD AMENDMENT
by Burnham Holmes

THE FOURTH AMENDMENT
by Paula A. Franklin

THE FIFTH AMENDMENT
by Burnham Holmes

THE SIXTH AMENDMENT
by Eden Force

THE SEVENTH AMENDMENT
by Lila E. Summer

THE EIGHTH AMENDMENT
by Vincent Buranelli

THE NINTH AMENDMENT
by Philip A. Klinkner

THE TENTH AMENDMENT
by Judith Adams

The Bill of Rights

AMENDMENT 1*
Article Congress shall make no law respecting an establishment of religion, or prohibiting the free exercise thereof; or abridging the freedom of speech, or of the press; or the right of the people peaceably to assemble, and to petition the Government for a redress of grievances.

AMENDMENT 2
Article A well regulated Militia, being necessary to the security of a free State, the right of the people to keep and bear Arms, shall not be infringed.

AMENDMENT 3
Article No Soldier shall, in time of peace be quartered in any house, without the consent of the Owner, nor in time of war, but in a manner to be prescribed by law.

AMENDMENT 4
Article The right of the people to be secure in their persons, houses, papers, and effects, against unreasonable searches and seizures, shall not be violated, and no Warrants shall issue, but upon probable cause, supported by Oath or affirmation, and particularly describing the place to be searched, and the persons or things to be seized.

AMENDMENT 5
Article No person shall be held to answer for a capital, or otherwise infamous crime, unless on a presentment or indictment of a Grand Jury, except in cases arising in the land or naval forces, or in the Militia, when in actual service in time of War or public danger; nor shall any person be subject for the same offence to be twice put in jeopardy of life or limb; nor shall be compelled in any criminal case to be a witness against himself, nor be deprived of life, liberty, or property, without due process of law; nor shall private property be taken for public use without just compensation.

AMENDMENT 6
Article In all criminal prosecutions, the accused shall enjoy the right to a speedy and public trial, by an impartial jury of the State and district wherein the crime shall have been committed, which district shall have been previously ascertained by law, and to be informed of the nature and cause of the accusation; to be confronted with the witnesses against him; to have compulsory process for obtaining Witnesses in his favor, and to have the assistance of counsel for his defence.

AMENDMENT 7
Article In Suits at common law, where the value in controversy shall exceed twenty dollars, the right of trial by jury shall be preserved, and no fact tried by a jury, shall be otherwise reexamined in any Court of the United States, than according to the rules of the common law.

AMENDMENT 8
Article Excessive bail shall not be required, nor excessive fines imposed, nor cruel and unusual punishments inflicted.

AMENDMENT 9
Article The enumeration in the Constitution, of certain rights, shall not be construed to deny or disparage others retained by the people.

AMENDMENT 10
Article The powers not delegated to the United States by the Constitution, nor prohibited by it to the States, are reserved to the States respectively, or to the people.

*Note that each of the first ten amendments to the original Constitution is called an "Article." None of these amendments had actual numbers at the time of their ratification.

TIME CHART

THE HISTORY OF THE
BILL OF RIGHTS

1770s–1790s

1774 Quartering Act
1775 Revolutionary War begins
1776 Declaration of Independence is signed.
1783 Revolutionary War ends.
1787 Constitutional Convention writes the U.S. Constitution.
1788 U.S. Constitution is ratified by most states.
1789 Congress proposes the Bill of Rights
1791 The Bill of Rights is ratified by the states.
1792 Militia Act

1800s–1820s

1803 *Marbury* v. *Madison*. Supreme Court declares that it has the power of judicial review and exercises it. This is the first case in which the Court holds a law of Congress unconstitutional.
1807 Trial of Aaron Burr. Ruling that juries may have knowledge of a case so long as they have not yet formed an opinion.
1813 Kentucky becomes the first state to outlaw concealed weapons.
1824 *Gibbons* v. *Ogden*. Supreme Court defines Congress's power to regulate commerce, including trade between states and within states if that commerce affects other states.

1830s–1870s

1833 *Barron* v. *Baltimore.* Supreme Court rules that Bill of Rights applies only to actions of the federal government, not to the states and local governments.

1851 *Cooley* v. *Board of Wardens of the Port of Philadelphia.* Supreme Court rules that states can apply their own rules to some foreign and interstate commerce if their rules are of a local nature—unless or until Congress makes rules for particular situations.

1857 *Dred Scott* v. *Sandford.* Supreme Court denies that African Americans are citizens even if they happen to live in a "free state."

1862 Militia Act

1865 Thirteenth Amendment is ratified. Slavery is not allowed in the United States.

1868 Fourteenth Amendment is ratified. All people born or naturalized in the United States are citizens. Their privileges and immunities are protected, as are their life, liberty, and property according to due process. They have equal protection of the laws.

1873 *Slaughterhouse* cases. Supreme Court rules that the Fourteenth Amendment does not limit state power to make laws dealing with economic matters. Court mentions the unenumerated right to political participation.

1876 *United States* v. *Cruikshank.* Supreme Court rules that the right to bear arms for a lawful purpose is not an absolute right granted by the Constitution. States can limit this right and make their own gun-control laws.

1880s–1920s

1884 *Hurtado* v. *California.* Supreme Court rules that the right to a grand jury indictment doesn't apply to the states.

1896 *Plessy* v. *Ferguson.* Supreme Court upholds a state law based on "separate but equal" facilities for different races.

1903 Militia Act creates National Guard.

1905 *Lochner* v. *New York.* Supreme Court strikes down a state law regulating maximum work hours.

1914 *Weeks* v. *United States.* Supreme Court establishes that illegally obtained evidence, obtained by unreasonable search and seizure, cannot be used in federal trials.

1918 *Hammer* v. *Dagenhart.* Supreme Court declares unconstitutional a federal law prohibiting the shipment between states of goods made by young children.

1923 *Meyer* v. *Nebraska.* Supreme Court rules that a law banning teaching of foreign languages or teaching in languages other than English is unconstitutional. Court says that certain areas of people's private lives are protected from government interference.

1925 *Carroll* v. *United States.* Supreme Court allows searches of automobiles without a search warrant under some circumstances.

1925 *Gitlow* v. *New York.* Supreme Court rules that freedom of speech and freedom of the press are protected from state actions by the Fourteenth Amendment.

1931 *Near* v. *Minnesota*. Supreme Court rules that liberty of the press and of speech are safeguarded from state action.

1931 *Stromberg* v. *California*. Supreme Court extends concept of freedom of speech to symbolic actions such as displaying a flag.

1932 *Powell* v. *Alabama* (*First Scottsboro* case). Supreme Court rules that poor defendants have a right to an appointed lawyer when tried for crimes that may result in the death penalty.

1934 National Firearms Act becomes the first federal law to restrict the keeping and bearing of arms.

1935 *Norris* v. *Alabama* (*Second Scottsboro* case). Supreme Court reverses the conviction of an African American because of the long continued excluding of African Americans from jury service in the trial area.

1937 *Palko* v. *Connecticut*. Supreme Court refuses to require states to protect people under the double jeopardy clause of the Bill of Rights. But the case leads to future application of individual rights in the Bill of Rights to the states on a case-by-case basis.

1937 *DeJonge* v. *Oregon*. Supreme Court rules that freedom of assembly and petition are protected against state laws.

1939 *United States* v. *Miller*. Supreme Court rules that National Firearms Act of 1934 does not violate Second Amendment.

1940 *Cantwell* v. *Connecticut*. Supreme Court rules that free exercise of religion is protected against state laws.

1943 *Barnette* v. *West Virginia State Board of Education*. Supreme Court rules that flag salute laws are unconstitutional.

1946 *Theil* v. *Pacific Railroad*. Juries must be a cross section of the community, excluding no group based on religion, race, sex, or economic status.

1947 *Everson* v. *Board of Education*. Supreme Court rules that government attempts to impose religious practices, the establishment of religion, is forbidden to the states.

1948 *In re Oliver*. Supreme Court rules that defendants have a right to public trial in nonfederal trials.

1949 *Wolf* v. *California*. Supreme Court rules that freedom from unreasonable searches and seizures also applies to states.

1954 *Brown* v. *Board of Education of Topeka*. Supreme Court holds that segregation on the basis of race (in public education) denies equal protection of the laws.

1958 *NAACP* v. *Alabama*. Supreme Court rules that the privacy of membership lists in an organization is part of the right to freedom of assembly and association.

1960s

1961 *Mapp* v. *Ohio*. Supreme Court rules that illegally obtained evidence must not be allowed in state criminal trials.

1962 *Engel* v. *Vitale*. Supreme Court strikes down state-sponsored school prayer, saying it is no business of government to compose official prayers as part of a religious program carried on by the government.

1963 *Gideon* v. *Wainwright*. Supreme Court rules that the right of people accused of serious crimes to be represented by an appointed counsel applies to state criminal trials.

1964 Civil Rights Act is passed.

1964 *Malloy* v. *Hogan*. Supreme Court rules that the right to protection against forced self-incrimination applies to state trials.

1965 *Griswold* v. *Connecticut*. Supreme Court rules that there is a right to privacy in marriage and declares unconstitutional a state law banning the use of or the giving of information about birth control.

1965 *Pointer* v. *Texas*. Supreme Court rules that the right to confront witnesses against an accused person applies to state trials.

1966 *Parker* v. *Gladden*. Supreme Court ruling is interpreted to mean that the right to an impartial jury is applied to the states.

1966 *Miranda* v. *Arizona*. Supreme Court extends the protection against forced self-incrimination. Police have to inform people in custody of their rights before questioning them.

1967 *Katz* v. *United States*. Supreme Court rules that people's right to be free of unreasonable searches includes protection against electronic surveillance.

1967 *Washington* v. *Texas*. Supreme Court rules that accused people have the right to have witnesses in their favor brought into court.

1967 *In re Gault*. Supreme Court rules that juvenile proceedings that might lead to the young person's being sent to a state institution must follow due process and fair treatment. These include the rights against forced self-incrimination, to counsel, to confront witnesses.

1967 *Klopfer* v. *North Carolina*. Supreme Court rules that the right to a speedy trial applies to state trials.

1968 *Duncan* v. *Louisiana*. Supreme Court rules that the right to a jury trial in criminal cases applies to state trials.

1969 *Benton* v. *Maryland*. Supreme Court rules that the protection against double jeopardy applies to the states.

1969 *Brandenburg* v. *Ohio*. Supreme Court rules that speech calling for the use of force or crime can only be prohibited if it is directed to bringing about immediate lawless action and is likely to bring about such action.

1970s–1990s

1970 *Williams* v. *Florida*. Juries in cases that do not lead to the possibility of the death penalty may consist of six jurors rather than twelve.

1971 *Pentagon Papers* case. Freedom of the press is protected by forbidding prior restraint.

1971 *Duke Power Co.* v. *Carolina Environmental Study Group, Inc.* Supreme Court upholds state law limiting liability of federally licensed power companies in the event of a nuclear accident.

1972 *Furman* v. *Georgia*. Supreme Court rules that the death penalty (as it was then decided upon) is cruel and unusual punishment and therefore unconstitutional.

1972 *Argersinger* v. *Hamlin*. Supreme Court rules that right to counsel applies to all criminal cases that might involve a jail term.

1973 *Roe* v. *Wade*. Supreme Court declares that the right to privacy protects a woman's right to end pregnancy by abortion under specified circumstances.

1976 *Gregg* v. *Georgia*. Supreme Court rules that the death penalty is to be allowed if it is decided upon in a consistent and reasonable way, if the sentencing follows strict guidelines, and if the penalty is not required for certain crimes.

1976 *National League of Cities* v. *Usery*. Supreme Court holds that the Tenth Amendment prevents Congress from making federal minimum wage and overtime rules apply to state and city workers.

1981 *Quilici* v. *Village of Morton Grove*. U.S. district court upholds a local ban on sale and possession of handguns.

1985 *Garcia* v. *San Antonio Metropolitan Transit Authority*. Supreme Court rules that Congress can make laws dealing with wages and hour rules applied to city-owned transportation systems.

1989 *Webster* v. *Reproductive Health Services*. Supreme Court holds that a state may prohibit all use of public facilities and publicly employed staff in abortions.

1989 *Johnson* v. *Texas*. Supreme Court rules that flag burning is protected and is a form of "symbolic speech."

1990 *Cruzan* v. *Missouri Department of Health*. Supreme Court recognizes for the first time a very sick person's right to die without being forced to undergo unwanted medical treatment and a person's right to a living will.

1990 *Noriega–CNN* case. Supreme Court upholds lower federal court's decision to allow temporary prior restraint thus limiting the First Amendment right of freedom of the press.

The Birth of the Bill of Rights

"We hold these truths to be self-evident, that all men are created equal, that they are endowed by their Creator with certain unalienable Rights, that among these are Life, Liberty, and the pursuit of Happiness."

THE DECLARATION OF INDEPENDENCE (1776)

A brave Chinese student standing in front of a line of tanks, Eastern Europeans marching against the secret police, happy crowds dancing on top of the Berlin Wall—these were recent scenes of people trying to gain their freedom or celebrating it. The scenes and the events that sparked them will live on in history. They also show the lasting gift that is our Bill of Rights. The freedoms guaranteed by the Bill of Rights have guided and inspired millions of people all over the world in their struggle for freedom.

The Colonies Gain Their Freedom

Like many countries today, the United States fought to gain freedom and democracy for itself. The American colonies had a revolution from 1775 to 1783 to free themselves from British rule.

The colonists fought to free themselves because they believed that the British had violated, or gone against, their rights. The colonists held what some considered the extreme idea that all

James Madison is known as both the "Father of the Constitution" and the "Father of the Bill of Rights." In 1789 he proposed to Congress the amendments that became the Bill of Rights. Madison served two terms as president of the United States from 1809 to 1817.

The Raising of the Liberty Pole by John McRae. In 1776, American colonists hoisted liberty poles as symbols of liberty and freedom from British rule. At the top they usually placed a liberty cap. Such caps resembled the caps given to slaves in ancient Rome when they were freed.

persons are born with certain rights. They believed that these rights could not be taken away, even by the government. The importance our nation gave to individual rights can be seen in the Declaration of Independence. The Declaration, written by Thomas Jefferson in 1776, states:

> We hold these truths to be self-evident, that all men are created equal, that they are endowed by their Creator with certain unalienable Rights, that among these are Life, Liberty, and the pursuit of Happiness.

The United States won its independence from Britain in 1783. But with freedom came the difficult job of forming a government. The Americans wanted a government that was strong enough to keep peace and prosperity, but not so strong that it might take away the rights for which the Revolution had been fought. The Articles of Confederation was the country's first written plan of government.

The Articles of Confederation, becoming law in 1781, created a weak national government. The defects in the Articles soon became clear to many Americans. Because the United States did not have a strong national government, its economy suffered. Under the Articles, Congress did not have the power to tax. It had to ask the states for money or borrow it. There was no separate president or court system. Nine of the states had to agree before Congress's bills became law. In 1786 economic problems caused farmers in Massachusetts to revolt. The national government was almost powerless to stop the revolt. It was also unable to build an army or navy strong enough to protect the United States's borders and its ships on the high seas.

The Constitution Is Drawn Up

The nation's problems had to be solved. So, in February 1787, the Continental Congress asked the states to send delegates to a convention to discuss ways of improving the Articles. That May, fifty-five delegates, from every state except Rhode Island, met in Philadelphia. The group included some of the country's most famous leaders: George Washington, hero of the Revolution; Benjamin Franklin, publisher, inventor, and diplomat; and James Madison, a leading critic of the Articles. Madison would soon become the guiding force behind the Constitutional Convention.

After a long, hot summer of debate the delegates finally drew up the document that became the U.S. Constitution. It set up a strong central government. But it also divided power between three branches of the federal government. These three branches were the executive branch (the presidency), the legislative branch (Congress), and the judicial branch (the courts). Each was given one part of the government's power. This division was to make sure that no single branch became so powerful that it could violate the people's rights.

The legislative branch (made up of the House of Representatives and the Senate) would have the power to pass laws, raise taxes and spend money, regulate the national economy, and declare war. The executive branch was given the power to carry out the laws, run foreign affairs, and command the military.

The Signing of the Constitution painted by Thomas Rossiter. The Constitutional Convention met in Philadelphia from May into September 1787. The proposed Constitution contained protection for some individual rights such as protection against *ex post facto* laws and bills of attainder. When the Constitution was ratified by the required number of states in 1788, however, it did not have a bill of rights.

The role of the judicial branch in this plan was less clear. The Constitution said that the judicial branch would have "judicial power." However, it was unclear exactly what this power was. Over the years "judicial power" has come to mean "judicial review." The power of judicial review allows the federal courts to reject laws passed by Congress or the state legislatures that they believe violate the Constitution.

Judicial review helps protect our rights. It allows federal courts to reject laws that violate the Constitution's guarantees of individual rights. Because of this power, James Madison believed that the courts would be an "impenetrable bulwark," an unbreakable wall, against any attempt by government to take away these rights.

The Constitution did more than divide the power of the federal government among the three branches. It also divided power between the states and the federal government. This division of power is known as *federalism*. Federalism means that the federal

government has control over certain areas. These include regulating the national economy and running foreign and military affairs. The states have control over most other areas. For example, they regulate their economies and make most other laws. Once again, the Framers (writers) of the Constitution hoped that the division of powers would keep both the states and the federal government from becoming too strong and possibly violating individual rights.

The new Constitution did *not*, however, contain a bill of rights. Such a bill would list the people's rights and would forbid the government from interfering with them. The only discussion of the topic came late in the convention. At that time, George Mason of Virginia called for a bill of rights. A Connecticut delegate, Roger Sherman, disagreed. He claimed that a bill of rights was not needed. In his view, the Constitution did not take away any of the rights in the bills of rights in the state constitutions. These had been put in place during the Revolution. The other delegates agreed with Roger Sherman. Mason's proposal was voted down by all.

Yet the Constitution was not without guarantees of individual rights. One of these rights was the protection of *habeas corpus*. This is a legal term that refers to the right of someone who has been arrested to be brought into court and formally charged with a crime. Another right forbade *ex post facto* laws. These are laws that outlaw actions that took place before the passage of the laws. Other parts of the Constitution forbade bills of attainder (laws pronouncing a person guilty of a crime without trial), required jury trials, restricted convictions for treason, and guaranteed a republican form of government. That is a government in which political power rests with citizens who vote for elected officials and representatives responsible to the voters. The Constitution also forbade making public officials pass any "religious test." This meant that religious requirements could not be forced on public officials.

The Debate Over the New Constitution

Once it was written, the Constitution had to be ratified, or approved, by nine of the states before it could go into effect. The new

Constitution created much controversy. Heated battles raged in many states over whether or not to approve the document. One of the main arguments used by those who opposed the Constitution (the Anti-Federalists) was that the Constitution made the federal government too strong. They feared that it might violate the rights of the people just as the British government had. Although he had helped write the Constitution, Anti-Federalist George Mason opposed it for this reason. He claimed that he would sooner chop off his right hand than put it to the Constitution as it then stood.

To correct what they viewed as flaws in the Constitution, the Anti-Federalists insisted that it have a bill of rights. The fiery orator of the Revolution, Patrick Henry, another Anti-Federalist, exclaimed, "Liberty, the greatest of all earthly blessings—give us that precious jewel, and you may take every thing else!"

Although he was not an Anti-Federalist, Thomas Jefferson also believed that a bill of rights was needed. He wrote a letter to James Madison, a wavering Federalist, in which he said: "A bill of rights is what the people are entitled to against every government on earth."

Supporters of the Constitution (the Federalists) argued that it did not need a bill of rights. One reason they stated, similar to that given at the Philadelphia convention, was that most state constitutions had a bill of rights. Nothing in the Constitution would limit or abolish these rights. In 1788 James Madison wrote that he thought a bill of rights would provide only weak "parchment barriers" against attempts by government to take away individual rights. He believed that history had shown that a bill of rights was ineffective on "those occasions when its control [was] needed most."

The views of the Anti-Federalists seem to have had more support than did those of the Federalists. The Federalists came to realize that without a bill of rights, the states might not approve the new Constitution. To ensure ratification, the Federalists therefore agreed to support adding a bill of rights to the Constitution.

With this compromise, eleven of the thirteen states ratified the Constitution by July 1788. The new government of the United States was born. The two remaining states, North Carolina and

Rhode Island, in time accepted the new Constitution. North Carolina approved it in November 1789 and Rhode Island in May 1790.

James Madison Calls for a Bill of Rights

On April 30, 1789, George Washington took the oath of office as president. The new government was launched. One of its first jobs was to amend, or change, the Constitution to include a bill of rights. This is what many of the states had called for during the ratification process. Leading this effort in the new Congress was James Madison. He was a strong supporter of individual rights. As a member of the Virginia legislature, he had helped frame the Virginia Declaration of Rights. He had also fought for religious liberty.

Madison, however, had at first opposed including a bill of rights. But his views had changed. He feared that the Constitution would not be ratified by enough states to become law unless the Federalists offered to include a bill of rights. Madison also knew that many people were afraid of the new government. He feared they might oppose its actions or attempt to undo it. He said a bill of rights "will kill the opposition everywhere, and by putting an end to disaffection to [discontent with] the Government itself, enable the administration to venture on measures not otherwise safe."

On June 8, 1789, the thirty-eight-year-old Madison rose to speak in the House of Representatives. He called for several changes to the Constitution that contained the basis of our present Bill of Rights. Despite his powerful words, Madison's speech did not excite his listeners. Most Federalists in Congress opposed a bill of rights. Others believed that the new Constitution should be given more time to operate before Congress considered making any changes. Many Anti-Federalists wanted a new constitutional convention. There, they hoped to greatly limit the powers of the federal government. These Anti-Federalists thought that adding a bill of rights to the Constitution would prevent their movement for a new convention.

Finally, in August, Madison persuaded the House to consider

his amendments. The House accepted most of them. However, instead of being placed in the relevant sections of the Constitution, as Madison had called for, the House voted to add them as separate amendments. This change—listing the amendments together—made the Bill of Rights the distinct document that it is today.

After approval by the House, the amendments went to the Senate. The Senate dropped what Madison considered the most important part of his plan. This was the protection of freedom of the press, freedom of religious belief, and the right to trial by jury from violation by the states. Protection of these rights from violation by state governments would have to wait until after the Fourteenth Amendment was adopted in 1868.

The House and the Senate at last agreed on ten amendments to protect individual rights. What rights were protected? Here is a partial list:

The First Amendment protects freedom of religion, of speech, of the press, of peaceful assembly, and of petition.

The Second Amendment gives to the states the right to keep a militia (a volunteer, reserve military force) and to the people the right to keep and bear arms.

The Third Amendment prevents the government from keeping troops in private homes during wartime.

The Fourth Amendment protects individuals from unreasonable searches and seizures by the government.

The Fifth Amendment states that the government must get an indictment (an official ruling that a crime has been committed) before someone can be tried for a serious crime. This amendment bans "double jeopardy." This means trying a person twice for the same criminal offense. It also protects people from having to testify against themselves in court.

The Fifth Amendment also says that the government cannot take away a person's "life, liberty, or property, without due process of law." This means that the government must follow fair and just procedures if it takes away a person's "life, liberty, or property." Finally, the Fifth Amendment says that if the government takes property from an individual for public use, it must pay that person an adequate sum of money for the property.

The Sixth Amendment requires that all criminal trials be speedy and public, and decided by a fair jury. The amendment also allows people on trial to know what offense they have been charged with. It also allows them to be present when others testify against them, to call witnesses to their defense, and to have the help of a lawyer.

The Seventh Amendment provides for a jury trial in all cases involving amounts over $20.

The Eighth Amendment forbids unreasonably high bail (money paid to free someone from jail before his or her trial), unreasonably large fines, and cruel and unusual punishments.

The Ninth Amendment says that the rights of the people are not limited only to those listed in the Bill of Rights.

Finally, the Tenth Amendment helps to establish federalism by giving to the states and the people any powers not given to the federal government by the Constitution.

After being approved by the House and the Senate, the amendments were sent to the states for adoption in October 1789. By December 1791, three-fourths of the states had approved the ten amendments we now know as the Bill of Rights. The Bill of Rights had become part of the U.S. Constitution.

How Our Court System Works

Many of the events in this book concern court cases involving the Bill of Rights. To help understand how the U.S. court system works, here is a brief description.

The U.S. federal court system has three levels. At the lowest level are the federal district courts. There are ninety-four district courts, each covering a different area of the United States and its territories. Most cases having to do with the Constitution begin in the district courts.

People who lose their cases in the district courts may then appeal to the next level in the court system, the federal courts of appeals. To appeal means to take your case to a higher court in an attempt to change the lower court's decision. Here, those who are making the appeal try to obtain a different judgment. There are thirteen federal courts of appeals in the United States.

People who lose in the federal courts of appeals may then take their case to the U.S. Supreme Court. It is the highest court in the land. The Supreme Court has the final say in a case. You cannot appeal a Supreme Court decision.

The size of the Supreme Court is set by Congress and has changed over the years. Since 1869 the Supreme Court has been made up of nine justices. One is the chief justice of the United States, and eight are associate justices. The justices are named by the president and confirmed by the Senate.

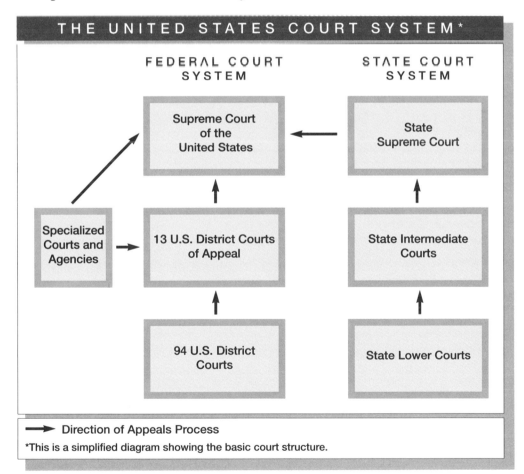

THE UNITED STATES COURT SYSTEM*

FEDERAL COURT SYSTEM — STATE COURT SYSTEM

Supreme Court of the United States

State Supreme Court

Specialized Courts and Agencies

13 U.S. District Courts of Appeal

State Intermediate Courts

94 U.S. District Courts

State Lower Courts

Direction of Appeals Process

*This is a simplified diagram showing the basic court structure.

In the Supreme Court, a simple majority of votes is needed to decide a case. If there is a tie, the lower court's decision remains in effect. When the chief justice votes on the majority side, he or she can assign the writing of the opinion to any of the majority justices, including himself or herself. The opinion states the Court's decision and the reasons for it. Who writes the opinion when the chief justice hasn't voted on the majority side? In that case, the longest-serving associate justice who voted for the majority decision can assign the writing to any of the majority justices, including himself or herself.

What if a justice has voted for the majority decision but doesn't agree with the reasons given in the majority opinion? He or she may write what is called a concurring opinion. That is one which agrees with the Court's decision but for different reasons.

Those justices who disagree with the Court's decision may write what is called a dissenting opinion. They have the opportunity to explain why they think the majority Supreme Court decision is wrong.

In addition to the federal court system, each state has its own system of courts. These systems vary from state to state. However, they are usually made up of two or three levels of lower courts and then the state's highest court, usually called the state supreme court. Those who lose their cases in the state supreme court may appeal those decisions to the federal court system, usually to the Supreme Court.

Not all cases that are appealed to the Supreme Court are heard by it. In fact, very few of them are. For the Supreme Court to decide to hear a case, four of the nine justices must vote to hear it. If fewer than four justices vote to hear the case, then the judgment of the lower court remains in effect.

The Third Amendment

The practice of illegally quartering soldiers (providing lodging for them) in people's homes had been outlawed in England during the late seventeenth century. Nevertheless, when England fought the French and Indian War in America, British troops often needed lodging. In addition, after the British won that war, they left behind a huge standing army in the colonies.

It was the presence of these 10,000 British troops that quickly led to the Quartering Acts and eventually to the colonists' fear that private homes would be used to house soldiers. The story that unfolds on the following pages is the development of the Third Amendment—the protection against the quartering of soldiers in private homes during peacetime without the owner's consent or during wartime except when allowed by law.

PHILIP A. KLINKNER

The English Attitude Toward Quartering Soldiers

"The poorest man may in his cottage bid defiance to all the force of the Crown. It may be frail; its roof may shake; the wind may blow through it; the storms may enter, the rain may enter—but the King of England cannot enter; all his forces dare not cross the threshold of the ruined tenement."

WILLIAM PITT THE ELDER

These words were not spoken by an American patriot. They were not the thoughts of a Thomas Paine, a Samuel Adams, or a Thomas Jefferson. They were spoken by the English statesman and orator William Pitt the Elder. Delivering a speech before the British Parliament—the lawmaking body—during the late 1700s, Pitt was talking about the security of the home.

The idea of the protection of rights under the law wasn't new to the colonists of the eighteenth century. In fact, it was part of the English constitutional tradition. The great documents of this legal tradition were the Petition of Right (1628) and the English Bill of Rights (1689). Both were giant strides taken by the House of Commons—the lower house of Parliament—to limit the power of the king. These two important documents also addressed the need to limit the king's use of soldiers to enforce his will throughout the land.

The English Parliament made sure that King William and Queen Mary agreed to the English Bill of Rights before they were crowned as England's new monarchs in 1689. The English Bill of Rights declared illegal the maintaining of a permanent army without the consent of Parliament.

The Petition of Right in 1628

The many problems raised by the quartering of soldiers was something that had long been understood in England. *Quartering* means providing lodging for troops. Much earlier, the English themselves had objected to the practice of quartering soldiers in private homes.

In the Petition of Right, Parliament had in 1628 protested to King Charles I the practice of quartering soldiers in private homes. This was how Parliament stated its objection to quartering military personnel:

Charles I ruled as king of England from 1625 to 1649. In 1628, Parliament tried to limit the authority of the king by passing the Petition of Right. Among its requests was one that soldiers and sailors should not be housed in people's homes. But from 1629 to 1640 Charles I ruled the country without a Parliament. After a bitter civil war, the king was tried and sentenced to death. Charles I was beheaded in 1649.

And whereas of late, great companies of soldiers and mariners [sailors] have been dispersed into divers [various] counties of the realm, and the inhabitants against their wills have been compelled to receive them into their houses, and there to suffer them to sojourn [stay] against the laws and customs of this realm and to the great grievance and vexation [irritation] of the people.

The solution proposed by Parliament wasn't a complex one. It was simply to stop the practice: "They do therefore humbly pray . . . that your Majesty would be pleased to remove the said soldiers and mariners, and that your people may not be so burdened in time to come. . . ."

In addition to protesting the quartering of the military, Parliament's petition also addressed other important issues. Among them were the use of martial law, forced loans and taxes, and imprisonment without stating the cause. The Petition of Right was the first time that Parliament had ever tried to limit the authority of the king.

The English Bill of Rights in 1689

The next time that Parliament would set forth a document to limit royal authority was in 1689. The document was the English Bill of Rights, which stated: "Whereas the late King James the Second, by the assistance of divers evil councilors, judges, and ministers employed by him, did endeavor [try] to subvert [overturn] . . . the laws and liberties of the kingdom [England]."

Something new that was introduced by the English Bill of Rights was the objection to a standing army during peacetime. A standing army is a permanent army of paid soldiers. One of the problems with keeping a large standing army was that it was very expensive. Taxes would have to be raised in order to support the military. Another problem was the impact of such an army on the mood of the people. It often made people very fearful to have a large number of soldiers among them.

English soldiers during the reign of Charles I of England.

The U.S. Bill of Rights has many of its roots in the English Bill of Rights. The part of that document that relates to our Third Amendment states that King James II tried to overturn "the laws and liberties of the Kingdom. . . .By raising and keeping a standing army within this kingdom in time of peace without consent of Parliament and quartering soldiers contrary to law. . . ."

A Problem of the English

One of the problems that led to England's and America's conflict during the revolutionary war was that the English seemed to have forgotten the ideas stated in the Petition of Right and their own Bill of Rights. There was a long-standing rejection of the quartering of soldiers in English history. Yet when it came to the English-speaking colonies across the Atlantic, the British wanted to quarter their soldiers in barracks, other buildings, and, in a few cases, private homes.

Another problem that seemed to go unrecognized by the English was that many colonists were originally from England. The colonists had learned to dislike the quartering of soldiers in people's homes while they were living in England. Just because they were now living in the colonies did not mean that they would accept quartering any more readily.

James Otis and the Writs of Assistance

You can hear the colonial American's dislike of quartering soldiers in the plea of James Otis of Boston as he argued against writs of assistance in 1761. A writ of assistance was a government document that enabled customs officials to search for smuggled goods wherever they wanted to do so. If necessary, they could ask for help from anyone in the area. That is why they are called writs of assistance. (King George III wanted new writs of assistance that would allow these officials in charge of customs—taxes on imported goods—to raise more money to help pay for the costs of a recent war.)

"Now one of the most essential branches of English liberty is the freedom of one's house," declared Otis. "A man's house is his castle; and whilst he is quiet, he is as well guarded as a prince in his castle. This writ, if it should be declared legal, would totally annihilate [destroy] this privilege."

William Pitt the Elder (1708–1778). In the late 1760s and in the 1770s, he protested against British policies in the American colonies.

A Sympathetic View from the Other Side

One person who would not accept the British attitude toward the colonists was William Pitt the Elder. Pitt, also known as the earl of Chatham, sided with the Americans not only on the issue of quartering soldiers but also on the issues of standing armies and taxation. He understood what it was like to have a large standing army on one's native soil. This is evident in a speech that Pitt made on November 18, 1777: "If I were an American, as I am an Englishman, while a foreign troop was landed in my country I never would lay down my arms,—never! never! never!"

How the French and Indian War Led to the Quartering Act of 1765

"[C]ivil officers . . . are hereby required to billet and quarter the officers and soldiers, in his Majesty's service, in the barracks provided by the colonies."

The Quartering Act of 1765

British troops were first quartered, or housed, in America during the French and Indian War. This war began in 1754 and plunged Britain and France into a nine-year-long conflict. The prize was control of the Ohio Valley.

A soldier's life was dangerous and uncomfortable. After marching about twenty miles a day toward the next battle, troops had to find shelter as night approached. During good weather, British troops could sleep outdoors in tents. But when the weather was bad, soldiers, especially officers, were sometimes quartered in private homes for the night.

Not only was a soldier's life rough, but the soldiers themselves were rough and tough. Poorly educated and poorly paid, they sometimes even had criminal backgrounds. Some people would call them "the dregs of society." To maintain order among the troops, discipline was often severe.

American colonists in Boston protest against British policies, 1765. The British needed money to help pay for their victory in the long war against the French, which had ended in 1763. The British also wanted to keep a large peacetime military force in their colonies. The colonists resented the new taxes and the attempts to quarter troops in barracks in the colonies.

"During the two winters last past," stated a court petition from Princeton, New Jersey, during the 1700s, colonists "have been obliged to quarter in their houses, some two, some three, others four of his majesty's troops. . . ." Having troops staying in their homes did create both a physical and financial burden for the colonists. But it was not until the tensions between Britain and the colonies became much worse that there was widespread resistance to quartering.

The years of war brought out several differences between the British and the French. England had more soldiers in North America than the French did. The English navy was stronger. Finally, England had more money to spend on the war.

However, the French did have certain strengths. They knew the backwoods. French traders and trappers were experts at canoeing streams and rivers. They knew the trails that connected the French outposts in the Ohio Valley. In addition, the French got along better with the Native Americans. The French had been trading for furs with them for many years. They seemed to have an appreciation and understanding of each other.

Even after the French and Indian War ended, the idea sprang up to keep British troops in North America. The English general Thomas Gage convinced the British government of the need to keep a large standing army in the colonies. After the Treaty of Paris (1763) officially brought the war to a close, William Pitt the Elder, supported a bill for the funds to carry out this plan. Though ailing, Pitt helped speed the legislation through Parliament so fast that people said it practically "stole through the House."

Why did the British government want to leave a standing army of 10,000 troops in the colonies even though peace had been achieved? Did the government fear that either the French or especially the Native Americans would once again take up arms, or that the Spanish would attack from the south? The British were less than confident that the colonists would be able to keep such an uprising or attack in check. Did the British fear that the colonists themselves would be the ones to start an uprising? The presence of

British troops would help make certain that the Americans remained faithful subjects to the English king.

Whatever the reason, the British left behind a large standing army in the colonies. The headquarters of the British military was to be located in New York City. The commander in chief would be General Thomas Gage.

The terms of the Treaty of Paris made England the major power in North America. From France, England received Canada and all the land east of the Mississippi River except for the port of New Orleans. England received Florida from Spain and in exchange gave the island of Cuba to the Spanish. France gave the land west of the Mississippi to Spain and kept only two small islands near Newfoundland.

General Gage's area of control was huge. It spread from Newfoundland in the north to Florida in the south and went as far east as the islands of Bermuda. To the west, it ranged from the Great Lakes to the Mississippi. It would be difficult for any single group or individual to journey the length and breadth of this vast landscape. It would be even more difficult to try to control it with an army.

General Thomas Gage

Who was this English officer who would play such an important role in America's colonial history?

Gage was born into a wealthy family. He began his army career at the age of twenty and served as an aide-de-camp to the earl of Albemarle during the War of the Austrian Succession. He also took part in the Battle of Culloden during the Scottish uprising in 1745. By 1751, Gage had been promoted to lieutenant colonel. He was transferred to Virginia in 1754.

As an officer under General Edward Braddock, commander of the British forces in America, Gage was responsible for the advance column as Braddock's forces marched from Virginia to Fort Duquesne in Pennsylvania. One of the volunteer officers was none other than twenty-three-year-old Colonel George Washington. While crossing the Monongahela River, the British forces were caught totally by surprise by the French and their Native American allies. The advance column, responsible for preventing a surprise attack, had failed in its task. Gage showed courage and a cool head under fire, as he and his men fought back. But the British were firing into the trees with little success. Gage was wounded twice, and his unit was almost destroyed. All the same, he was able to put together a rear guard of eighty men to cover Braddock's retreat. Many of the troops were killed during the retreat, including General Braddock. Washington escaped with only thirty of his men. Although his coat had been shot through and through, Washington was uninjured.

In 1756, the person who took Braddock's place made an observation about Thomas Gage. "Lt Col Gage is a good Officer and keeps up Discipline Strictly," wrote the earl of Loudoun, the new commander in chief. "The Regt is in Rags but look like Soldiers."

General Edward Braddock, commander in chief of British forces in North America, was surprised by an attack of French and Native American forces and defeated at the battle of the Monongahela in 1755. Braddock died of the wounds he received there. George Washington, in his early twenties, also took part in the fighting.

The earl of Loudoun seems to have given a fair assessment of Thomas Gage. He wasn't a stirring leader in the field. Nor was he a shrewd master of tactics studying maps in the glow of lantern light. Gage was fond of details. He would probably have made a better quartermaster, performing the difficult task of furnishing rations and equipment to the troops. Instead, he was a rising young commander of British forces in America.

One of the major problems of the British army was fighting in the woods. Sometimes the soldiers seemed to be engaged in combat with the dark trees and the sounds of the night rather than with the enemy. The colonists were often better adapted to fighting in the forests. For this reason they sometimes served as scouts for the British troops.

Responding to the challenge, Gage organized—at his own expense—a unit of light infantry trained for this type of fighting. Instead of standing upright and motionless in long firing lines, these riflemen were trained in a different type of warfare. They darted in and out in quick skirmishes, or small fights, scouted territory behind enemy lines, and set up outposts to discover the enemy's movements. The soldiers were from the colonies, and the officers were from England. Gage was the commander. The generals took notice of Gage's efforts and promoted him to colonel.

Colonel Gage led his light infantry unit during a frontal attack against the French at Fort Ticonderoga. The attack was a dismal failure in which many British soldiers were killed. Gage was wounded again.

In the fall of 1758, Gage was promoted to brigadier general. At the time, he was serving under General Jeffrey Amherst in military action against Montreal. Amherst had positioned Gage as the rear guard, a position where attention to detail could prove more important than decision making under fire. When the fighting was over, the entire province of Quebec had surrendered to the British.

In 1761, Gage was appointed to the rank of major general. He was also made the military governor of Montreal. During this period, Gage married Margaret Kemble, a young woman from the

General Thomas Gage served as commander in chief of British forces in North America from 1763 to 1773. He strongly favored a law giving him the right to quarter troops in barracks and other buildings.

colony of New Jersey. This marriage gave him a closer tie with America than most Englishmen had.

In 1763, Major General Thomas Gage succeeded General Jeffrey Amherst. Gage was now the commander in chief of all the British forces in the colonies. In spite of all the success he achieved, however, Gage's military career seemed to be marked by a real lack of distinction. It might be said of Thomas Gage that his major talents were for waiting things through, not suffering out-and-out disasters, and being in the right place at the right time.

Events Leading to the Quartering Act

When General Gage was governor of Montreal, there had been no barracks for the British troops. Soldiers had been quartered in private homes. However, the situation in Montreal had been different from that in Massachusetts and other colonies. In Montreal quartering had been forced on an enemy population during a time of war.

Gage pushed for quartering when he spoke to the British government about the problems of housing troops in America. George Grenville, the prime minister of England in 1764, realized that the quartering issue would prove to be a big problem. It was "by far the most likely to create difficulties and uneasiness," Grenville said, ". . . especially as the quartering of soldiers upon the people against their wills is declared by the petition of right to be contrary to law." Here, of course, Grenville was referring to England's Petition of Right (1628).

What General Gage seems to have been most worried about was the prospect of difficulties in housing troops when they were on the march from one barracks to another. There would be times when troops might find themselves in areas where there were few inns or public houses available. Also, Gage was probably worried that the colonists might have a change of heart. During the French and Indian War, they had always been more or less willing to go along with the army's requests. But what if that were to stop? General Gage wanted to have the legal backing to take action in case the situation changed.

Despite Gage's anxieties, a solution to the problem of housing troops had been worked out during the French and Indian War. In 1758, Benjamin Franklin wrote a plan for the governor of Pennsylvania that helped to solve the local housing problem. Instead of being housed in private homes, soldiers were placed in rented buildings that served as barracks. It was this idea that Grenville examined closely as he tried to find the solution to the problem of housing British troops in the colonies.

What Grenville proposed to do was to take these *voluntary* practices and make a law that would *require* the colonies to continue to do what they were already doing. The result was the Quartering Act. This act was first passed by the British Parliament on March 24, 1765, and renewed every year.

The Quartering Act of 1765

The Quartering Act of 1765 stated in part that "civil officers . . . within his Majesty's dominions [lands] in *America* . . . are hereby required to billet [to assign lodging by a billet, or official order] and quarter the officers and soldiers, in his Majesty's service, in the barracks provided by the colonies; and . . . to quarter and billet the residue [those remaining] of such officers and soldiers for whom there shall not be room in such barracks, in inns, livery [horse] stables, . . . [and] victualling-houses [eating houses]. . . ."

But the demands of the Quartering Act did not stop there. It also stated "[t]hat all such officers and soldiers, so put and placed in such barracks . . . shall, from time to time, be furnished and supplied there . . . with fire, candles, vinegar, and salt, bedding, utensils [knives, forks, and spoons] for dressing their victuals [food] . . . to each man without paying any thing for the same. . . ."

John Dickinson, a speaker of the Delaware assembly in 1760 and a member of the Pennsylvania assembly from 1762 to 1765, wrote a series of letters in which he commented on the issues of the day. One of the incidents that sparked Dickinson's letter writing was the Quartering Act. In one of his letters, Dickinson said:

> If the *British* parliament has legal authority to issue an order that we shall furnish a single article for the troops here, and to compel obedience to *that* order, they have the same right to issue an order for us to supply those troops with arms, cloth[e]s, and every

necessary; and to compel obedience to *that* order also; in short, to lay any burthens [burdens] they please upon us. What is this but taxing us at a certain sum, and leaving to us only the manner of raising it? How is this mode more tolerable than the Stamp Act?

What the colonists objected to was the compulsory nature of the Quartering Act—that is, the fact that it *required* them to provide housing and small items for the troops. As Dickinson pointed out, there was no real difference between being required to provide these things and being required to pay a tax.

The Stamp Act of 1765

The Stamp Act was another one of Grenville's ideas. Its purpose was to raise money for the British treasury. Stamps would be needed for such items as newspapers, pamphlets, legal documents, almanacs, ships' papers, licenses, and other public papers. Grenville had "hoped that the power and sovereignty [rule] of Parliament, over every part of the British dominions, for the purpose of raising or collecting any tax, would never be disputed."

Grenville's hopes were unrealistic. And this was soon demonstrated. Even before the stamps arrived in Boston, New York City, and other colonial towns, gangs of angry protesters roamed the streets. Later they picked fights with stamp agents sent to enforce the Stamp Act. Lawyers, publishers, and merchants—those mainly affected by the act—didn't mind seeing the "Liberty Boys" tangling with the British troops.

During the Stamp Act crisis, Gage behaved responsibly, ordering the British troops to fire on protesters only in self-defense. The public outcry continued, however. By the fall of 1765, every stamp agent had been forced to quit. Parliament, faced with having a law that it couldn't enforce, repealed, or canceled, the Stamp Act in 1766. In time, tempers cooled. But although the crisis over the Stamp Act may have quieted down, the colonists' dislike of British policies would live on.

CHAPTER 3

How the Quartering of British Troops Led to the Boston Massacre

"... if the troops attempt to quarter in the town, I greatly fear the consequence."

A Bostonian

The first opposition to the Quartering Act took place in New York. In 1766, the New York Assembly voted to follow all the requirements of the Quartering Act except for providing such supplies as salt and vinegar. They stated that they could not afford to furnish 1,100 soldiers with supplies.

The British struck back swiftly. Governor Henry Moore dismissed the New York Assembly. The civil governors of the colonies were appointed by the king of England. One of the primary duties of a governor was to veto, or reject, any local laws that were not in the interests of the Crown.

The British Parliament declared all business carried out by the New York Assembly to be null and void—that is, without legal force. For a time, the British even thought about making it a crime to write or speak out against the Quartering Act. All trials of these cases would be held in England.

British troops enter Boston on October 1, 1768. Some of the troops at first moved into tents pitched on Boston Common. Others found temporary quarters at Faneuil Hall and at the Town House, the meeting place of the local government. Still other troops moved into rented warehouses.

John Dickinson's response to the actions of the British was loud and clear: "If the Parliament may lawfully deprive New York of any of her rights, it may deprive any, or all the other colonies. . . . He certainly is not a wise man who folds his arms and reposes [rests] himself at home, viewing with unconcern the flames that have invaded his neighbour's house, without using any endeavors [attempts] to extinguish them."

Dickinson's letter-essays caused quite a stir as they were passed from reader to reader. They were published as a series in newspapers and later published as a pamphlet entitled *Letters from a Farmer in Pennsylvania to the Inhabitants of the British Colonies.*

The Quartering of Soldiers in Boston

Francis Bernard, the governor of Massachusetts, didn't want British troops quartered in New England either. In 1766, he wrote a letter stating his belief "that they should not be quarter'd in the old Colonies which have been long settled and inhabited, unless call'd for by the Civil Magistrate or Government of the Province, as necessary to preserve the publick [public] peace."

But Governor Bernard's wish was not to be. After the Stamp Act riots in Boston, it was decided that two regiments of British troops would be sent there. On September 3, 1768, General Gage sent Captain William Shirreff for secret talks with Governor Bernard about where the troops would be quartered. They decided that one regiment would be quartered in Castle William, a fortress on one of the harbor islands, and one regiment would be quartered in town. Governor Bernard made it clear to General Gage that it should appear to be the general's decision. Otherwise, Governor Bernard said, the town council would "advise me to Quarter them all at the Castle."

When the troop commander, Lieutenant Colonel William Dalrymple, arrived to discuss the quartering of his soldiers, Governor Bernard tried to convince him that Castle William was still legally within the limits of Boston. The colonel, however, was less

John Dickinson, an American lawyer and politician, attended the 1765 Stamp Act Congress to protest British policies. He publicized his protests further in a series of letters in 1767 and 1768 entitled *Letters from a Farmer in Pennsylvania to the Inhabitants of the British Colonies.*

than happy. If his command was split apart, he could not be responsible for what might happen in the town. Besides, Boston and Castle William "certainly were distinct in his orders; . . . he was not used to dispute his Orders but obey them & therefore should most certainly march his Regiment into the Town."

The next day General Gage sent another officer, Captain John Montresor, to Boston. Captain Montresor warned Governor Bernard that the people of Boston seemed to be on the verge of rioting over the troops' arrival. The captain then announced that both regiments would be quartered in the town of Boston.

On October 1, 1768, column after column of British troops left the fleet of nine ships anchored in Boston Harbor. There were two regiments, the Fourteenth and the Twenty-ninth. Each had nine companies of soldiers. In addition, there was one company of artillerymen and another group of eighty-four men from the Fifty-ninth Regiment.

With flags flying and drummers drumming, the soldiers paraded into Boston, which had about 16,000 people. It was quite a sight for the townspeople. The soldiers wore three-cornered black hats, and the grenadiers (soldiers armed with grenades) wore high black beaver hats. Since they had no quarters yet, the Twenty-ninth Regiment pitched their tents in the midst of curious onlookers on Boston Common, a public park. Until the snows and winter winds came, the soldiers would be relatively comfortable.

It was suggested that the rest of the soldiers live at the Manufactory House. But families were already living there, and they wouldn't move. Temporary quarters were then found for the Fourteenth Regiment at a public market called Faneuil Hall and in Boston Town House, the meeting place of the local government. It was not lost on the likes of radical patriots such as Samuel Adams, Paul Revere, and James Otis that the Redcoats were sleeping in the town's house of government.

General Gage arrived in Boston and ordered Governor Bernard to find permanent quarters for the troops. This time Thomas Hutchinson, who was both lieutenant governor and chief justice, tried the Manufactory House with no success. After a while, vacant warehouses in the area around the Custom House were rented out for the quartering of soldiers. To show how unfocused the issue of quartering was at this point, consider the ownership of the warehouses. One of the warehouses rented to the troops belonged to William Molyneux, a member of the Sons of Liberty (the radical group of patriots led by Samuel Adams). Another warehouse belonged to Nathaniel Wheelwright, a prominent Whig (a patriotic American colonist who later supported the Revolution).

Having the British troops living right in the hub of Boston would change things dramatically. Tensions were beginning to rise. One observer presented the mood of the day in this way: "At present, people do not seem disposed to resist the troops, but their tempers are in such a ferment [turmoil] that they may be easily pushed on to the most desperate measures; and if the troops attempt to quarter in the town, I greatly fear the consequence." These words proved to be an accurate forecast of what was to come.

The Boston Massacre

It was a Monday night. The ringing of bells could be heard. The sound of church bells at night usually meant that a fire was raging somewhere in town. But on the night of March 5, 1770, things were very different. There was no fire.

Day after day in early March, fights had broken out between a group of ropemakers and British soldiers. Off-duty soldiers often sought out extra work among local businesses to boost their poor military pay. They could usually find work at Gray's Ropewalk twisting the long strands of hemp into rope. Some of the ill will between the British soldiers and the American workers grew from the fact that the soldiers were willing to work for very low wages.

Word quickly traveled along the narrow streets surrounding Gray's Ropewalk that something big was brewing and would soon boil over. Suddenly men and boys poured out of doors. Some carried clubs. Others held on to wouldrings—the wooden paddles used in ropemaking. One or two even sported bats, borrowed from a game similar to stickball called tipcat.

Walking and running toward the Custom House, the crowd swelled to around 300. At King Street, they met six British soldiers under the command of Captain Thomas Preston. The crowd quickly turned into a mob. Jeering at the soldiers and taunting them, the mob dared the British to fire. The soldiers stood their ground. Sticks were thrown, knocking off the soldiers' hats and thudding against their muskets. Captain Preston pleaded with the crowd to go home, but he was greeted with catcalls and snowballs.

The colonists moved forward. The soldiers defended themselves with the bayonets that attached to the ends of their double-loaded muskets. Captain Preston may never have issued the command to shoot. Perhaps someone in the mob yelled "fire!" Or perhaps the soldiers simply snapped. Many of them had already been pressed to the breaking point by the unruly colonists.

Suddenly a single shot was fired. What came to be called the Boston Massacre had begun. The first shot was quickly followed by another. At other times the British had loaded their muskets only with gunpowder to make lots of noise in an attempt to quiet things down. But not this time. A Bostonian tumbled to the ground. Another man crumpled in the street. A boy clutched his leg, crying out in pain. The cold air was filled with plumes of white smoke and the sharp burn of gunpowder. Panic-stricken, the mob began to zigzag away into the darkness.

Three Bostonians died on the streets that night. Two died later, and six more were wounded. Several of the dead and injured were teenagers. But the number of dead and wounded might easily have skyrocketed. The Sons of Liberty had been joined by the local militia and farmers from the surrounding countryside. Throughout the night, crowds greatly outnumbering the British troops milled about and emotions reached a fever pitch. Lieutenant Governor Thomas Hutchinson made a speech to the angry Bostonians promising that there would be a murder trial. Fortunately for everyone, there were no more face-to-face meetings that night between the British and the Bostonians.

The next day, an investigation determined that the death of a man mistakenly identified as Michael Johnson had been caused by two musket balls "which were shot thro' his body." Not until some hours later was the dead man correctly identified. The first person to be killed in the Boston Massacre was an African American named Crispus Attucks.

The Aftermath

The tensions, of course, did not relax after the Boston Massacre. The people of Boston still ran into British troops marching through the winding streets. The anger of the Bostonians only grew at the sight of these Redcoats. If the townspeople chose to clear their heads in the sea breeze, they could see the British man-of-war ships that ringed the harbor. It was said that the big guns on these ships could send a cannonball over the town of Boston to nearby Charlestown.

For many Bostonians, especially the Sons of Liberty, the upcoming trial of the British soldiers involved in the Boston Massacre did nothing to calm the situation. Samuel Adams called a town meeting to demand the removal of British troops from Boston. In response, Lieutenant Governor Hutchinson called for one regiment to leave their quarters in Boston. When that did not quiet the protests of the people, Hutchinson sent the second regiment to join

The Boston Massacre, March 5, 1770. Many of the colonists in Boston resented the presence of troops in their city. They called the red-coated soldiers "lobsterbacks" and had them arrested for breaking local laws whenever they could. The tensions led to violence and the deaths of five civilians, which a local newspaper immediately called a "BLOODY MASSACRE."

the first one in Castle William. The British troops would no longer be quartered in Boston. Instead, they would be living three miles away on Castle Island.

The Importance of the Trial

The day after the Boston Massacre, no British lawyer could be found to defend the soldiers before a jury of colonists. However, one of the town's leading patriot lawyers, Josiah Quincy, Jr., said he would represent the soldiers if John Adams would join him. John Adams, the cousin of Samuel Adams, took little time to decide. John Adams believed "that Council [legal help] ought to be the very last thing that an accused person should want [need] in a free country." He also saw this case "as important a cause as had ever been tried in any court or country of the world."

General Gage realized the political importance of the trial. "It is absolutely necessary everything relating to the unhappy affair of the 5th of March should appear as full as it is possible upon Captain Preston's tryal [trial]," wrote Gage in a letter to the commander of the garrison at Boston. "Not only what happened on the said night should be circumstantially [by detailed evidence] made to appear, but also every insult and attack made upon the troops previous thereto with the pains taken by the military to prevent quarrels between the soldiers and inhabitants."

"Hear Ye! Hear Ye!"

The Jurors for the said Lord the King upon oath present that Thomas Preston, Esq. (and others)...not having the fear of God before their eyes, but being moved and seduced [persuaded] by the instigation [urging] of the devil and their own wicked hearts, did on the 5th day of this instant March, at Boston...with force and arms feloniously [villainously], willfully and of their malice aforethought assault one Crispus Attucks...of which said mortal wounds the said Crispus Attucks then and there instantly died.

Thus began the original charge brought against the British soldiers by the people of Boston, However, early in the trial, John Adams's great skills as a lawyer were displayed. Adams requested that Preston be placed on trial separately from his men. The motion was granted. One by one, Adams then dismissed all eighteen would-be jurors because they were from Boston. The next group of jurors were from outside Boston.

The Trial of Captain Thomas Preston

At first Preston's trial seemed to be going the prosecution's way. Then Adams produced a surprise witness for the defense. Richard Palmes, a merchant of Boston, reluctantly took the witness stand. He told of how, on the night of March 5, he had spoken to Captain Preston as the soldiers stood in front of the angry mob.

"Sir," said Palmes, "I hope you don't intend the soldiers shall fire on the inhabitants. He said, 'by no means.' The instant he spoke I saw something resembling snow or ice strike the grenadier on the Captain's right hand, being the only one then at his right. [The soldier] instantly stepped one foot back and fired the first gun. . . ."

This testimony placed the events of that evening in a very different light. The mob's anger had been on the verge of spilling over into violence. Captain Preston had probably not even issued the command to fire.

Then, quoting from common law (law based on custom, usage, and court decisions) and Sir Edward Coke (a former English judge and law expert), the defense attorneys added layer after layer of cases to strengthen Captain Preston's claim of self-defense. In a situation of mob violence, who could blame Captain Preston? the attorneys asked. Wasn't he only acting in self-defense, as well as in the best interests of his men?

At this point it was the judges' turn. Dressed in their powdered white wigs and floor-length red robes (red was worn for a murder trial), the judges pointed out that Captain Preston probably had not commanded the soldiers to fire. Even if he had, they said, he did so for a good reason: to protect his own life and the lives of his soldiers.

It took only three hours for the jury to decide. Captain Preston was found not guilty. Upon hearing the verdict, Preston left by boat for Castle William and was never seen again on the streets of Boston.

The Trial of the Six Soldiers

During the trial of the soldiers, the prosecution tried to show that the soldiers had been the aggressors. The defense, on the other hand, unfolded a different story about what happened on the night of the Boston Massacre.

"Did they crowd near the soldiers?" asked Josiah Quincy, Jr., one of the defense lawyers.

"So near, that I think you could not get your hat betwixt [between] them and the bayonets," answered Nathaniel Russell, a chairmaker.

"How many people do you think there might be in the whole?" continued Quincy.

"About two hundred," replied Russell.

"Did the soldiers say anything to the people?"

"They never opened their lips; they stood in a trembling manner, as if they expected nothing but death."

Another defense witness told of the conduct of Crispus Attucks. He said Attucks held the musket of one of the soldiers with one hand and beat the soldier around the head with the other. Attucks then yelled, "Kill the dogs."

The most damaging defense witness for the prosecution's case was Doctor John Jeffries. This widely respected physician had treated Patrick Carr, a Bostonian who was shot that night and died nine days later. On the witness stand, Jeffries said:

He told me that he thought that the soldiers would have fired long before. I then asked him if he thought the soldiers would have been hurt if they had not fired. He said he really thought they would, for he had heard many voices cry out "Kill them." I asked him then, meaning to close all, whether he thought they fired in self-defense or on purpose to destroy the people. He said he really thought they did fire to defend themselves; that he did not blame the man, whoever he was, who shot him.

John Adams won acquittal, a verdict of not guilty, for all but two of the soldiers. Their punishment for manslaughter (the unlawful but unintentional killing)? Before being released, both read a passage from the Bible and were branded on their thumbs.

For his successful defense of the British soldiers, John Adams was thought by some to have betrayed the cause of the patriots. In spite of this, however, Adams went on to become one of the signers of the Declaration of Independence. Then, in 1797, this lawyer from Boston who had taken on an unpopular case became the second president of the United States.

The clock could never be turned back. "From that moment," declared Daniel Webster, an American lawyer and statesman, "we may date the severence [cutting apart] of the British Empire." As one season gave way to another, as one year fell into the next, the colonists and the British appeared to be marching double time, headlong toward each other.

CHAPTER 4

How Colonial Reaction to British Policy in North America Led to the American Revolution

". . . the Governor of the Province may order such uninhabited Houses, Outhouses, Barns, or other buildings, as he shall think necessary to be taken . . . and made fit for the Reception of such Officers and Soldiers, and quarter them therein, as he shall think proper."

The Second Quartering Act of 1774

The decision to keep a large standing army in colonial America helped to set in motion the events that would soon lead to the American Revolution. The money it cost to support the British troops made it necessary to tax the colonies. The Sugar Act of 1764, the Stamp Act of 1765, the Townshend Acts of 1767 (duties on imported goods such as glass, paint, lead, paper, and tea) were meant to raise money to pay for the standing army. These acts would, in time, lead to the battle cry of "No taxation without representation."

Little by little, Parliament ended every one of these special taxes except the one on tea. "What enforcing and what repealing; what bullying and what submitting; what doing and undoing," remarked Edmund Burke, the British statesman and political writer, about the House of Commons and its policy toward the colonies. Tea would play a large part in the events of 1773, as well as set the stage for later armed conflict.

The Boston Tea Party, December 16, 1773. Protesters dumped the tea from hundreds of chests into the harbor as crowds on shore watched. Although some colonial merchants denounced this destruction of property, most Bostonians supported the attack on British authority. Parliament soon passed harsh laws to punish Boston. These included a new Quartering Act.

The Boston Tea Party

Another battle cry was raised by a group of patriots dressed as Mohawk Indians on the night of December 16, 1773. This was an incident that lives on in the imagination of Americans. If this event had not actually happened, it would take a bold stroke of fiction to create the scene. Imagine bands of colonists outfitted as Native Americans moving under the cover of darkness toward the British tea ships anchored in the harbor.

The East India Company

Early in 1773, the East India Company (an English company holding a monopoly on the tea trade) was in financial trouble. To prevent its collapse, the British government allowed the company to have the sole right to sell tea in the colonies. There would be a tax of three pence per pound paid by the colonists. But the company would not have to pay English duties—taxes on imports. Most important, the tea would be cheaper than all other tea brought into the colonies either legally or illegally.

Even more than the tax, the idea of the monopoly angered the colonists. That November the *Dartmouth,* accompanied by two other tea ships, dropped anchor in Boston Harbor. The people of Boston would not allow the tea to be taken from the ships. Governor Thomas Hutchinson would not allow the ships to leave the harbor until the duty on the tea had been paid. So there the three ships stood at anchor, carrying a cargo that could not be unloaded and sails that could not be hoisted for a return voyage to England.

The Effect of the Quartering Policy

The policy of quartering soldiers on Castle Island in Boston Harbor had a direct effect on the events of that night. The soldiers were too far away to prevent the colonists from dumping the tea. If the British troops had still been quartered in town, the results of that evening would probably have been very different. In fact, the

A colonial American silver tea service. The Boston Tea Party of 1773 was not the only protest against the Tea Act. In April 1774, people disguised as Native Americans dumped a cargo of tea into New York Harbor. In October, a ship and its tea cargo were burned at Annapolis, Maryland. In December, protesters burned tea stored in Greenwich, New Jersey.

colonists probably would not even have tried their bold rebellion.

The absence of British soldiers also had another effect. The people of Boston strolled down to the harbor to watch in silence. If the British troops had been stationed in Boston, they could have kept the townspeople away. Then Admiral Montagu could have fired the long-range guns.

That night, Admiral Montagu noticed the turmoil in the harbor. If there had not been so many innocent civilians watching, the

British could have responded with an artillery barrage. However, the British weren't willing to have another massacre. Also, this one would have been on a far greater scale.

The Boston Tea Party: Who Was There?

Who were the Bostonians dressed up as Mohawks who crept aboard the ships that night? Even John Adams, who seemed to know everyone and everything in Boston worth knowing, wasn't sure. Of course, there would have been some members of the Sons of Liberty, along with some of the other active patriots of the day. But for some reason—no one knows quite why—it has always remained a secret. But you can probably bet that Paul Revere was on deck or below. Revere seemed to be everywhere in and around Boston, doing everything.

The Significance

An ax cracked open the one remaining tea chest. After a final heave-ho, the last of the 342 tea chests splashed into the dark, salty water below. The three groups of men, one on each ship, had emptied the three ships of their cargo in just under three hours. Boston Harbor had been turned into one giant teapot, steeping in tea.

The significance of the Boston Tea Party did not escape the notice of John Adams. "This Destruction of the Tea is so bold," observed Adams, "so daring, so firm, intrepid, & inflexible, and it must have so important Consequences and so lasting, that I cannot but consider it as an Epocha [an event that begins a new period] in History. . . ."

The Aftermath: The Intolerable Acts

To punish the colonies for their actions, the British Parliament reacted swiftly and firmly. Ignoring the objections of Edmund

Burke in the House of Commons and William Pitt in the House of Lords, the British lawmakers passed a series of highly restrictive acts. These were known as the Intolerable Acts.

The first of these harsh measures was the Boston Port Bill of March 31, 1774. With the enforcement of this act, the British stopped "the landing and discharging, lading or shipping, of goods, wares, and merchandise, at the town, and within the harbour, of Boston, in the province of Massachuset[t]'s Bay, in North America." The port of Boston would not be reopened until the East India Company had been paid for the tea dumped into the sea and the customs had also been paid on that tea.

With Boston Harbor closed, Marblehead and Salem became the closest ports for shipping to Boston. But Bostonians were beginning to wage an economic war of their own. They were not only refusing to buy but even to use British goods. Other colonies quickly came to the aid of Massachusetts by supplying it with needed provisions.

The next two acts, passed on May 20, 1774, did away with certain freedoms that Bostonians had come to regard as essential. The Massachusetts Government Act tightened British rule by strengthening the power of the governor, controlling the appointments of officials and judges to the government of Boston, and by limiting town meetings to one per year. The Administration of Justice Act permitted the transfer of certain trials, such as those for capital crimes that occurred when holding down a riot or collecting taxes, to other provinces and even back to England.

The Quebec Act, passed on June 22, 1774, gave full legal rights to the Roman Catholics living in the eastern part of Canada. This angered the mostly Protestant population living along the Atlantic coast. The Quebec Act also extended the territory of Quebec south to the Ohio River. This area north and west of the Ohio River was land that Virginia, Connecticut, and Massachusetts had already claimed.

These first acts applied to the colonies of the Atlantic coast and primarily to Massachusetts. The British saw the coast of America as being more of a problem than the interior. Of course, the most troublesome spot of all was Boston.

A New Quartering Act

The last Intolerable Act was the infamous Quartering Act. The forerunner of this act, originally passed in 1765, had reached into the far corners of all the colonies. This was the reaction of Bostonians toward the quartering of soldiers, as stated in "A List of Infringements and Violations," drawn up at a public meeting at Faneuil Hall in Boston on October 28, 1772:

> Introducing and quartering standing armies in a free country in times of peace without the consent of the people either by themselves or by their representatives, is, and always has been deemed [believed] a violation of their rights as freemen; and of the charter or compact made between the King of Great Britain, and the people of this province, whereby all the rights of British subjects are confirmed to us.

In 1772, General Gage wrote about just these types of matters to the earl of Hillsborough:

> I find the Barrack Master will be obliged to supply the Company of the 31st Regiment in New-Providence, with Barrack Furniture and Utensils. Captain Hodgson, who commands said Company, has acquainted me, that Governor Shirley has done every thing in his Power, to procure them Bedding and Firewood with other Necessarys; but the Assembly pleaded the low State of the Treasury, and the Poverty of their Constituents, and agreed to supply the Troops only with oyl [oil] and Candles.

Since 1765, the Quartering Act had been renewed each year. In 1774, two Quartering Acts were passed. The second Quartering

Act that year allowed British commanders to locate their troops wherever they saw fit.

> [T]he Governor of the Province may order such uninhabited Houses, Outhouses, Barns, or other buildings, as he shall think necessary to be taken . . . and made fit for the Reception of such Officers and Soldiers, and quarter them therein, as he shall think proper.

This act was meant to stop the local authorities in Boston from quartering British troops in Castle William. The British no longer wanted their soldiers to live in the old fort on Castle Island in Boston Harbor: "And as it may frequently happen, from the Situation of such Barracks, that if Troops should be quartered therein, they would not be stationed where their Presence may be necessary and required." Instead, the British wanted their troops to be stationed in the center of the town of Boston.

British troops arriving in Boston in 1768 as shown in a 1770 engraving by Paul Revere. By 1774 a new Quartering Act permitted the troops to be quartered wherever the governor of Massachusetts thought "proper," including "other buildings" besides uninhabited houses and barns.

General Gage was the Englishman who put the new Quartering Act into practice. Part of his plan was to make the new laws absolutely intolerable to the colonists. He succeeded enormously in doing so. By forcing people to provide lodging and other supplies to enemy troops in their own inns, eating houses, and other buildings, Gage had not only increased their financial burden but also their anger.

Another important aspect of the Quartering Act is that it represented a war of wills between the king and the Parliament of England on the one side and the colonial legislatures of America on the other. In the first place, the colonists deeply resented England's practice of keeping large standing armies in America. In the second place, the colonists were offended by the British having such far-reaching powers to decide how and where these soldiers should be quartered.

The Quartering Act of 1774 did not openly state that soldiers could be quartered in private homes. However, the colonists feared that this might be the meaning of "other buildings." The colonists remained uncertain about the interpretation of this law by the British army, as well as by the government officials who were Tories (colonial Americans who remained loyal to England during the American Revolution). In effect, this raised the Quartering Act of 1774 to the level of a grievance held by the colonies against the British Crown.

After a visit to England and a discussion with George III, General Gage was no longer just the commander in chief of the British troops. He was now also the governor of Massachusetts. General-Governor Gage certainly had the chance to put his words and ideas into practice.

A Different Voice in Parliament

There were other very different views being voiced in Parliament. In the House of Lords, William Pitt spoke in favor of removing

British troops from the colonies. But his pleas fell on deaf ears. George III was headed in the opposite direction. In the winter of 1774, the king wrote to Pitt: "The New England governments are in a state of rebellion, blows must decide whether they are to be subject to this country or independent."

CHAPTER 5

The End and the Beginning

"If the British march
By land or sea from the town to-night,
Hang a lantern aloft in the belfry arch
Of the North Church tower as a signal light,—
One, if by land, and two, if by sea;
And I on the oposite shore will be,
Ready to ride and spread the alarm
Through every Middlesex village and farm,
For the country folk to be up and to arm."

HENRY WADSWORTH LONGFELLOW,
"PAUL REVERE'S RIDE," 1863

On April 18, 1775, General Thomas Gage sent 800 British troops on a twenty-mile march from Boston to Concord, Massachusetts. Their primary mission was to destroy the American military supplies there. A secondary mission was to capture John Hancock and Samuel Adams, two colonists thought to be dangerous to the Crown. They were reportedly staying at a house in Lexington, a town about halfway to Concord.

These secret plans had been discovered by Dr. Joseph Warren, a leading patriot. To warn the colonists of the approaching British troops, two horsemen rode hard out of Boston. Paul Revere, a silversmith and engraver, was rowed over to Charlestown. Then he rode to Medford and on to Lexington. William Dawes, a tanner, went by way of Boston Neck to Cambridge and on to Lexington. On their way to warn Hancock and Adams, the two horsemen also alerted the countryside all the way to Lexington.

Paul Revere rode to Lexington on the evening of April 18, 1775, to warn that British troops were coming. British troops captured Revere as he attempted to ride from Lexington to Concord. They let Revere go, however, and he returned to Lexington.

It was not long before the British troops realized that their secret had been found out. Colonel Francis Smith and Major John Pitcairn sent word back to Boston asking for reinforcements. Pitcairn moved ahead with a group of soldiers.

The Battle of Lexington

Early the next morning, Major Pitcairn and his men marched briskly into Lexington. Could it be that across the village green sixty to seventy men stood at the ready? The contrast was great. On one side were men in their splendid red uniforms; on the other side was a ragtag bunch of colonists. Surprisingly, these colonists (called Minutemen because they prided themselves on being ready

A 1775 engraving of the Battle of Lexington by Amos Doolittle. Major John Pitcairn directs the troops to fire upon the Minutemen.

in a minute) were lined up as if to fight. Barking out their instructions was a heavyset fellow named Captain John Parker.

Only a matter of moments had passed between Captain Parker's order to scatter and a volley of fire crackling from British muskets. No fewer than eight Minutemen lay dead. Ten others had been wounded. Stopping before Parson Clarke's house after the one-sided barrage, the Redcoats discovered that John Hancock and Samuel Adams were long gone.

The Battle of Concord

From Lexington, the British troops marched on to Concord. On their journey, the countryside sprang alive with resistance. At Concord, 500 Minutemen were waiting. The spirit of what happened next is recorded in the first stanza of Ralph Waldo Emerson's "Concord Hymn."

> By the rude bridge that arched the flood,
> Their flag to April's breeze unfurled,
> Here once the embattled farmers stood,
> And fired the shot heard round the world.

From everywhere, it seemed, British troops were being fired upon. The Minutemen would not let the British troops cross the North Bridge. The only smart thing for the troops to do was retreat. At Lexington, the backtracking Redcoats were joined by another 1,000 British troops under Lord Hugh Percy, a brigadier general from General Gage's staff. Two field artillery cannons were wheeled into place in an attempt to hold off the Minutemen. A local tavern was turned into a hospital for the many fallen Redcoats.

Lord Percy immediately sized up the situation. He fully understood how effective the Minutemen had been at Lexington. "They have men amongst them who know very well what they are about, having been employed as rangers against the Indians and Canadians," he wrote later. He was, of course, referring to the French and

Indian War. "And this country being much covered with wood, and hilly, is very advantageous for their method of fighting."

Later that day, the countryside once again fell quiet. The British had finally made it back to Boston. But along the return journey from Concord to Boston, the toll of British dead numbered 73, the number of wounded reached 174, and 26 were missing. On the American side, by contrast, 49 people lay dead, 39 had been wounded, and 5 missing.

Like a ship with its anchor hauled, men in the rigging and sails unfurled, the War for Independence was finally fully under way. There would be no turning back from its present course. From all over, men streamed into the area around Boston to join the new army. They came from as far away as Connecticut, Rhode Island, and New Hampshire.

George Washington and his troops watch as the British evacuate Boston on March 17, 1776.

General Thomas Gage also received reinforcements. One of them was a major general named William Howe. General Howe, a man beloved by his troops, would soon replace General Gage.

On March 17, 1776, the American forces under General George Washington drove the British troops out of Boston.

On the Road to Freedom

"For quartering large Bodies of Armed Troops among us . . ."
The Declaration of Independence, 1776

The Declaration of Independence of 1776 begins with a preamble, or general announcement, of the reasons for the document: "When in the Course of human Events, it becomes necessary for one People to dissolve the Political Bands which have connected them with another . . . a decent Respect to the Opinions of Mankind requires that they should declare the causes which impel [drive] them to the Separation."

The writer of the Declaration of Independence, Thomas Jefferson, then went on to list the abuses carried out by George III, the king of England. Among these abuses were the following:

"He has kept among us, in Times of Peace, Standing Armies, without the consent of our Legislature."

The practice of keeping standing armies during peacetime certainly violated the basic law of England—the English Bill of Rights (1689).

Thomas Jefferson headed the committee that prepared the Declaration of Independence. He wrote the first draft of the Declaration and presented it to Congress on July 2, 1776. Among the complaints against the British, the document listed the keeping of standing armies during peacetime without the consent of the lawmakers and the quartering of large numbers of troops.

"He has affected [acted] to render [make] the Military independent of and superior to the Civil Power."

Here Jefferson was referring to General Thomas Gage. In 1774, Gage became governor of Massachusetts. He was already the commander in chief of the British troops.

"He has combined with others to subject us to a Jurisdiction [authority of law] foreign to our Constitution, and unacknowledged by our Laws; giving his Assent [agreement] to their Acts of pretended Legislation."

Parliament passed laws for the colonies but without the right to do so and without holding the better interests of the colonies in mind.

"For quartering large Bodies of Armed Troops among us . . ."

With these words Jefferson could have been referring to many places, such as New York City, Boston, and Charleston, South Carolina.

"For protecting them, by a mock [fake] Trial, from Punishment for any Murders which they should commit on the Inhabitants of these States . . ."

Here Jefferson was referring to the trials of Captain Preston and his soldiers after the Boston Massacre. The Administration of Justice Act, one of the Intolerable Acts, would from 1774 onward protect soldiers who were carrying out their duty of preventing riots.

"For cutting off our Trade with all Parts of the World . . ."

Here Jefferson was referring to the Port of Boston Bill of 1774.

"For imposing [placing] Taxes on us without our Consent . . ."

Two of the major taxes passed were the Stamp Act of 1765 and the Revenue Act of 1767 (which imposed the "Townshend duties" on colonial imports of items such as glass, lead, paints, paper, and tea).

"For transporting us beyond Seas to be tried for pretended Offences . . ."

Jefferson was referring to the Administration of Justice Act.

This was the Intolerable Act that allowed certain trials to be moved to other provinces and even to England.

"For abolishing the free System of English Laws in a neighbouring Province, establishing therein an arbitrary [tyrannical] Government, and enlarging its Boundaries, so as to render it at once an Example and fit Instrument for introducing the same absolute Rule into these Colonies."

This complaint was about the Quebec Act of 1774.

From the Declaration of Independence to the Bill of Rights

The abuses listed in the Declaration of Independence anticipated the concerns dealt with in the Bill of Rights. The Second Amendment addresses the first two abuses concerning standing armies and the superiority of the military. The Third Amendment deals with the issue of quartering soldiers. Many of the other amendments were responses to the Intolerable Acts of 1774.

Members of Congress sign the Declaration of Independence.

The Colonies Speak Out Against Quartering

Massachusetts was not the only colony that opposed the quartering policies of the British. In 1776, Delaware set forth in its Declaration of Rights "that no soldier ought to be quartered in any house in time of peace without the consent of the owner, and in time of war in such a manner only as the Legislature shall direct." Later that same year, Maryland used similar words in its Declaration of Rights. Provisions against the quartering of soldiers were also included in the Massachusetts Declaration of Rights in 1780 and the New Hampshire Bill of Rights in 1783.

The British surrender at Yorktown, Virginia, on October 19, 1781. The official peace treaty was signed in 1783. By that year, protection against the quartering of troops without the consent of the people had been written into the state constitutions of Delaware, Maryland, Massachusetts, and New Hampshire. Not until ten years after the British surrendered was the federal Bill of Rights approved.

The End of the Journey

The American War of Independence would rage on until late 1781. The fighting stopped with the surrender of General William Cornwallis to General George Washington at Yorktown, Virginia, on October 19, 1781. The Treaty of Peace officially ending the war was signed on September 3, 1783. The era of quartering soldiers had come to an end.

CHAPTER 7

The Security of the Home

"No Soldier shall in time of peace be quartered in any house, without the consent of the Owner, nor in time of war, but in a manner to be prescribed by law."

Third Amendment

From the beginning of the French and Indian War to the end of the revolutionary war, Americans had often voluntarily agreed to house and feed troops of British and American soldiers. The colonists became angry only when they felt they were being forced to quarter soldiers. The colonists were also afraid they would be unprotected by proper legal safeguards and therefore be at the mercy of abuses by the military.

Housing and feeding soldiers against the will of the colonists and the lack of legal safeguards had become some of the leading complaints of the revolutionaries. These complaints, or grievances, led directly to the Third Amendment in the Bill of Rights.

The Relationship of the Third Amendment to Other Amendments

The quartering of soldiers in more recent years was prevented by the Third Amendment to the Bill of Rights in 1791. This amendment said it would no longer be permissible to quarter soldiers in

---

Today the Third Amendment protects Americans against the national government's quartering of troops in people's homes without their consent during peacetime.

private homes during peacetime. During wartime, the Third Amendment went on to state that it would take no less than an act of Congress to force the quartering of soldiers.

The Third Amendment grew out of the goal of keeping the military under civilian control. It is also associated with people's distrust of large standing armies. That is how it ties in with the Second Amendment.

The Second Amendment states: "A well regulated Militia, being necessary to the security of a free State, the right of the people to keep and bear Arms, shall not be infringed [violated]." Behind this amendment is the distrust of a large standing army and the yearning for a civilian army. In order to avoid the need for a large standing army, during times of crisis able-bodied men and women can be called up from the militia into active duty.

The Third Amendment can be seen as working hand in hand with the Fourth Amendment. The Fourth Amendment assures the "right of the people to be secure in their persons, houses, papers, and effects, against unreasonable searches and seizures." Having troops in the home, whether enemy or friendly, is a violation of this right.

The Third Amendment can also be viewed as a reflection of the First Amendment. "Congress shall make no law . . . abridging [reducing] the freedom of speech. . . ." Even in the privacy of your own home, it would be extremely difficult to talk freely and to read whatever you wanted to read if there were strangers watching and listening. If these people are within eyeshot or earshot, they may be noting what you read or say. What this amounts to is a violation of fundamental law and a type of thought police. Justice Thurgood Marshall of the Supreme Court once wrote: "A state has no business telling a man, sitting alone in his own house, what books he may read."

The Whisky Rebellion

The first crisis of the new United States occurred in 1794. Here is what happened. Farmers in western Pennsylvania were in the habit of using their leftover grain to make rye whiskey. In fact, whiskey even served as currency. In 1791, a tax was passed on liquor, but it was not being paid.

George Washington raised an army to march over the Allegheny Mountains and enforce the tax. Many of the men in this army had been too young to fight in the War of Independence and now wanted to fight for their country. Fifteen thousand joined, which was larger than the army Washington had led during most of the Revolution.

During the six-week march, the American army was careful not to quarter any troops. Every night tents were pitched for shelter until the army reached western Pennsylvania. Few tax violators were found, but it had been a real show of strength. There was no quartering of soldiers the whole time troops had been on the march.

Quartering During the Civil War

The Union army sometimes quartered troops during the Civil War. But the South had seceded (withdrawn from the United States), so there was no legal position that the Confederacy could take. Even so, the Union troops favored tents over quartering in private houses. Also, during Reconstruction the Union troops stayed in barracks rather than in private homes.

The Third Amendment in the Courts

Unlike some of the other amendments in the Bill of Rights, such as the Fifth Amendment, the Third Amendment is rarely mentioned in court cases. Two of the few cases took place in 1950 and 1982. These were the cases of *United States* v. *Valenzuela* and *Engblom* v. *Carey*.

The Case of *United States* v. *Valenzuela* (1950)

While Gus P. Valenzuela was in Korea in the armed services, the rental property he owned in Los Angeles fell under rent control.

Rent control is the regulation of the amount of rent a landlord may charge tenants. On April 6, 1950, Valenzuela, through his attorney, raised the issue of his protection under the Third Amendment.

Judge James M. Carter, a district judge in Los Angeles, responded in part in the following words:

> Reference will be made to only one of defendant's constitutional contentions. In his brief, the defendant states, "The 1947 House and Rent Act as amended and extended is and always was the incubator and hatchery of swarms of bureaucrats to be quartered as storm troopers upon the people in violation of Amendment III of the United States Constitution."
>
> "This challenge" to quote from defendant's brief, "has not been heretofore made or adjudged by any court, insofar as our research discloses."
>
> We accept counsel's statement as to the results of his research but find this challenge without merit.
>
> The motion to dismiss is denied.

In other words, Valenzuela was unable to prevent the rental property he owned from falling under the rent-control guidelines by claiming protection under the Third Amendment.

The Case of *Engblom* v. *Carey* (1982)

On April 18, 1979, a strike was called by the guards in the prisons of New York State. The governor of the state, Hugh L. Carey, forced the regular guards on strike to leave their rooms in staff housing buildings provided by the government. Their quarters were needed by their replacements, the soldiers of the National Guard.

Two of the striking guards, Marianne E. Engblom and Charles E. Palmer, brought suit against Governor Carey for his actions. Their argument in a case known as *Engblom* v. *Carey* was that this represented a quartering of soldiers during peacetime in direct violation of the Third Amendment.

Judge Irving R. Kaufman, judge of the United States Court of Appeals for the Second Circuit, who wrote the majority opinion in *Engblom* v. *Carey* (1982), ended the trial with these thoughts:

> After the Framers forged [formed] the Constitution, the memory of an oppressive military presence lingered among the people. Emanating [springing] from the first Congress in 1789 as part of the proposed Bill of Rights to meet the widespread popular demand for safeguards for individual rights and subsequently ratified by the States, the Third Amendment to the United States Constitution prohibited the often distrusted Federal Government from the peacetime quartering of soldiers in any house without the consent of the owner.
>
> With the help of the Fourth Amendment, the Third Amendment thus constitutionalized [set into constitutional terms] the maxim [saying], "every man's home is his castle." The Founding Fathers, I am certain, could not have imagined with this history that the Third Amendment could be used to prevent prison officials from affording necessary housing on their own property to those who were taking the place of striking guards.
>
> Although a man's home is his castle under the Third Amendment, it is not the case, as Gertrude Stein might say, that a house is a house is a house. [This was in reference to "a rose is a rose is a rose," the poet Gertrude Stein's way of countering an overly romantic view of the world.]
>
> A reasonable analysis of Engblom's and Palmer's possessory [possessive] interest in their rooms at the Mid-Orange Correctional Facility . . . support the district court's conclusion that Engblom and Palmer did not have the kind of property right that warrants [justifies] protection under the Third Amendment.

The Effect on Privacy

One of the influences of the Third Amendment today is in the field of privacy. In an important 1965 case dealing with the right to privacy and the use of birth control devices—*Griswold* v. *Connecticut*—the Supreme Court mentioned the Third Amendment. Supreme Court Justice William O. Douglas presented the Court's majority opinion. He referred to the Third Amendment and four other amendments in the Bill of Rights as "penumbras"—surrounding regions in which something exists—protecting the right to privacy. These "penumbras" are "formed by emanations [something spreading outward] from those guarantees that help give them life and substance." Justice Douglas's majority opinion said that the "Third Amendment in its prohibition against the quartering of soldiers 'in any house' in time of peace without the consent of the owner is another facet of that privacy."

Besides the Third Amendment, the following is a list of the other amendments the Supreme Court mentioned and the safeguard of each that throws off a "penumbra." The First Amendment protects the right of association. The Fourth Amendment guarantees protection against unreasonable search and seizure. The Fifth Amendment safeguards against self-incrimination. The Ninth Amendment establishes that the rights of the people are not just those stated in the Bill of Rights. According to Justice Douglas's majority opinion, the effect of the "penumbras" from these five different amendments is to "create zones of privacy."

A Last Look at Fundamental Law

A lasting aspect of the importance of the Third Amendment is that it is built on a cornerstone of fundamental law. This amendment has furthered Sir Edward Coke's basic belief that "a man's house is his castle." To make it more universal for humankind, a translation of the Latin following the previous quotation of Coke's states: "One's home is the safest refuge to everyone." No matter how humble, the home is a sanctuary. This is as true psychologically as it is physically. Robert Frost, the longtime state poet of Vermont and former poet laureate of the United States, once captured this idea in "The Death of the Hired Man":

" 'Home is the place where, when you have to go there,
    They have to take you in.' "

Is the Third Amendment Relevant Today?

A case is sometimes made for the opinion that the Third Amendment is a curiosity, merely a historical amendment. Those who argue in favor of this view often point to how this amendment served a purpose during a particular time and place. Today, however, they say it is largely irrelevant.

But who can predict the future? The events of the world seem to spin ever faster. It is possible that the day may come when the Third Amendment will again be needed as an active safeguard. Or, it might help prevent a related type of abuse.

So, even though the Third Amendment is to an extent a historical amendment, the same is true of the Declaration of Independence. This does not mean that the Declaration of Independence should be removed from its place of honor in American history. Nor should we dismiss the Third Amendment. Although it may play only a minor role in court trials today, this amendment still stands as a reminder of one of the most important safeguards in every American's life.

$\mathscr{I}$MPORTANT $\mathscr{D}$ATES

1628 Petition of Right in England includes Parliament's protest to King Charles I concerning the practice of quartering soldiers.

1689 English Bill of Rights includes Parliament's objection to King James II's practice of keeping a standing army and quartering soldiers.

1754 French and Indian War begins. Quartering of English soldiers first takes place in American colonies during this nine-year war.

1763 Treaty of Paris ending French and Indian War gives Britain land east of Mississippi River.

1763 England leaves a standing army of 10,000 soldiers in American colonies with headquarters in New York City. General Thomas Gage appointed commander.

1765 Quartering Act is passed and renewed every year until 1774.

1765 Stamp Act raises money for British treasury. Stamps needed for newspapers, pamphlets, licenses, and all public papers.

1766 First resistance to Quartering Act. New York Assembly votes not to provide troops with supplies. British Parliament suspends assembly.

1767 Townshend Acts place duties on imported goods.

1768 Boston replaces New York as headquarters of British army. Soldiers quartered in Boston.

1770 Quartering policy helps create tensions leading to Boston Massacre.

1770 Governor Thomas Hutchinson relocates British troops outside of Boston, three miles away on Castle Island in Boston Harbor.

1770 Trial of Captain Preston and six British soldiers who took part in Boston Massacre ends in their release.

1773 Boston Tea Party. Protest leads to Intolerable Acts.

1774 Boston Port Bill stops all shipping to and from Boston until duties paid on tea dumped into harbor and East India Company paid for its losses.

1774 Massachusetts Government Act tightens rule of British government by abolishing council and town meetings, as well as controlling appointments of officials and judges to Boston government.

1774 Administration of Justice Act permits transfer of certain trials to other provinces, as well as to England.

1774 Quebec Act extends territory of Quebec south to Ohio River and gives full legal rights to Roman Catholics living in province of Quebec.

1774 Two Quartering Acts in 1774. First is extension of original act passed in 1765. Second permits quartering of British troops wherever commander desires troops to be located.

1775 Battle of Lexington and Battle of Concord.

1776 George Washington drives British troops from Boston on March 17.

1776 Declaration of Independence on July 4 lists specific abuses of King George III. Abuses include: "He has kept among us, in Times of Peace, Standing Armies, without the consent of our Legislatures" and "For quartering large Bodies of Armed Troops among us."

1776 Delaware states in its Declaration of Rights "that no soldier ought to be quartered in any house in time of peace without the consent of the owner, and in time of war in such a manner only as the Legislature shall direct."

1781 Defeat of Cornwallis at Yorktown, Virginia.

1783 Peace treaty on September 3, officially ends American Revolution.

1789 On June 8, James Madison introduces Bill of Rights into the U.S. House of Representatives.

1789 On September 25, Congress proposes the amendments known as the Bill of Rights.

1791 On December 15, Virginia ratifies Bill of Rights. These amendments become official part of U.S. Constitution.

1794 George Washington sends army of 15,000 to stop Whiskey Rebellion. Government soldiers use tents rather than quartering during campaign.

1861–1865 Union army seldom uses quartering during Civil War. However, when quartering does occur, Southerners have no recourse in courts because the South has seceded from United States.

1950 *United States* v. *Valenzuela.* Gus P. Valenzuela, soldier in Korea, makes challenge before district court that rent-control act of Los Angeles violates his Third Amendment rights. His motion to dismiss proceedings is denied.

1982 *Engblom* v. *Carey.* Case of striking prison guards in New York State who lose their quarters to members of National Guard serving as their replacements until settlement of strike. Court decision is that the two guards do not have property rights that fall under the Third Amendment.

amendment   A change in the Constitution.

appeal   To refer a case to a higher court so that it will review the decision of a lower court.

bail   Money paid by the accused to gain his or her release in the period before trial to make sure he or she will show up for the trial. If the accused does not appear, he or she loses the money.

billet   An official order directing that a member of a military force be provided with food and lodging.

bill of attainder   A law pronouncing a person guilty of a serious crime without a trial.

concurring opinion   An opinion by one or more judges that agrees with the majority opinion but offers different reasons for reaching that decision.

customs   Taxes imposed by a government on goods brought into or sent out of a country.

defense   The party representing the accused individual.

dissenting opinion   An opinion by one or more judges that disagrees with the majority opinion.

double jeopardy   Putting a person on trial for a crime for which he or she has already been tried.

executive branch   The branch or part of the government that carries out the laws and makes sure they are obeyed.

ex post facto **law**   A law that makes illegal an action that took place before the law was passed.

federalism   The system by which the states and the federal government, each has certain special powers and shares others.

incorporation   The process of making Bill of Rights protections apply to the states so that people are safeguarded against state actions violating these rights.

indictment   A grand jury's written accusation that the person named has committed a crime.

judicial branch   The part or branch of the government that interprets the laws.

judicial review   The power of the courts to review the decisions of other parts or levels of the government. A court may review the decision of a lower court and come to a different decision.

legislative branch   The part or branch of the government that makes the laws.

majority opinion   The statement of a court's decision in which the majority of its members join.

precedent   A court decision that guides future decisions.

prosecution   The party pressing criminal charges on behalf of the government.

quartering   Providing living quarters—lodging—to members of a military force.

ratification   Approval of an amendment to the Constitution by three-fourths of state legislatures or conventions (after the amendment has been officially proposed by two-thirds of each house of Congress or proposed by a convention called by two-thirds of the states).

separation of powers   The division of the government into three parts or branches—the legislative, the executive, and the judicial.

standing army   A permanent army of paid soldiers.

writ of assistance   A written document issued by a government official allowing an officer to conduct an almost unlimited search and seizure and to ask for help in doing so.

$\mathscr{S}$UGGESTED $\mathscr{R}$EADING

Anderson, Fred. *A People's Army: Massachusetts Soldiers and Society in the Seven Years' War.* Chapel Hill: University of North Carolina Press, 1984.

*Athearn, Robert G. *Colonial America.* Vol. 2 of *American Heritage New Illustrated History of the United States.* New York: Fawcett, 1971.

*_____. *The Revolution.* Vol. 3 of *American Heritage New Illustrated History of the United States.* New York: Fawcett, 1971.

The Bill of Rights and Beyond: A Resource Guide. The Commission on the Bicentennial of the United States Constitution, 1990.

Carroll, Peter N., and David W. Noble. *The Restless Centuries: A History of the American People.* Vol. 1, *Colonial Times to 1877.* Minneapolis, Minn.: Burgess Publishing Co., 1973.

Colbourn, H. Trevor. *The Lamp of Experience: Whig History and the Intellectual Origins of the American Revolution.* Chapel Hill: University of North Carolina Press, 1965.

*Colby, Jean Poindexter. *Lexington & Concord, 1775: What Really Happened.* New York: Hastings House, 1975.

Donoughue, Bernard. *British Politics and the American Revolution: The Path to War, 1773–75.* London: Macmillan, 1964.

Gipson, Lawrence Henry. *The Coming of the Revolution: 1763–1775.* New York: Harper & Row, 1954.

Hansen, Harry. *The Boston Massacre: An Episode of Dissent and Violence.* New York: Hastings House, 1970.

Lancaster, Bruce, and J.H. Plumb. *The American Heritage Book of the Revolution.* New York: Dell, 1975.

Malone, Dumas. *The Story of the Declaration of Independence.* New York: Oxford University Press, 1975.

*Meltzer, Milton, ed. *The American Revolutionaries: A History in Their Own Words 1750–1800.* New York: Thomas Y. Crowell, 1987.

*Russell, Francis. *The French and Indian Wars.* New York: American Heritage, 1962.

*_____. *Lexington, Concord and Bunker Hill.* New York: American Heritage, 1963.

Scheer, George F., and Hugh F. Rankin. *Rebels and Redcoats.* New York: World Publishing Co., 1957.

Sosin, Jack M. *Agents and Merchants: British Colonial Policy and the Origins of the American Revolution, 1763–1775.* Lincoln: University of Nebraska Press, 1965.

Van Tyne, Claude H. *The Causes of the War of Independence.* Vol. 1, *The Founding of the American Republic.* New York: Peter Smith, 1951.

*Readers of *The Third Amendment* by Burnham Holmes will find these books particularly readable.

 OURCES

Carter, Clarence Edwin, ed. *The Correspondence of General Thomas Gage with the Secretaries of State,* vol. 1. New Haven: Yale University Press, 1931.

Commager, Henry Steele, ed. *Documents of American History.* 9th ed. Englewood Cliffs, N.J.: Prentice-Hall, 1973.

Dumbauld, Edward. *The Declaration of Independence and What It Means Today.* Norman: University of Oklahoma Press, 1950.

Federal Reporter, 2d ser., vol. 677. St. Paul, Minn.: West Publishing Co., 1982.

Federal Supplement, vol. 95. St. Paul, Minn.: West Publishing Co., 1951.

Fleming, Thomas J. "The Boston Massacre." In *Stories of Great Crimes & Trials.* New York: American Heritage Publishing Co., 1973.

Galvin, John R. *The Minute Men: A Compact History of the Defenders of the American Colonies 1645–1775.* New York: Hawthorne Books, 1967.

Great Britain Statutes, vol. 2. London: Charles Eyre and William Straham, printers, 1774.

The Guide to American Law: Everyone's Legal Encyclopedia. St. Paul, Minn.: West Publishing Co., 1984.

Jensen, Merrill. *The Founding of a Nation: A History of the American Revolution 1763–1776.* New York: Oxford University Press, 1968.

Larabee, Benjamin Woods. *The Boston Tea Party.* New York: Oxford University Press, 1964.

Miller, John C. *Origins of the American Revolution.* Boston: Little, Brown and Co., 1943.

Morgan, Edmund S. and Helen M. Morgan. *The Stamp Act Crisis.* Chapel Hill: University of North Carolina Press, 1953.

Morison, Samuel Eliot, ed. *Sources and Documents Illustrating the American Revolution, 1764–1788 and the Formation of Federal Constitution.* New York: Oxford University Press, 1965.

Morris, Richard B. *The American Revolution: A Short History.* Princeton, N.J.: D. Van Nostrand Company, 1955.

———. *The New World. Prehistory to 1774.* Vol. 1 of *The Life History of the United States.* New York: Time Inc., 1963.

———. *The Making of a Nation. 1775–1779.* Vol. 2 of *The Life History of the United States.* New York: Time Inc., 1963.

Robson, Eric. *The American Revolution: In Its Political and Military Aspects 1763–1783.* New York: W. W. Norton & Co., 1966.

Shy, John. *Toward Lexington: The Role of the British Army in the Coming of the American Revolution.* Princeton, N.J.: Princeton University Press, 1965.

Zobel, Hiller B. *The Boston Massacre.* New York: W. W. Norton & Co., 1970.

The Constitution of the United States

The original words of the Constitution are in the left-hand column. An easier-to-read version is in the right-hand column. Headings and numbers have been added to the easier version to make the meaning clearer. But, of course, the easier-to-read version is not as precise as the original and should be used simply to get the general ideas of the more complex original. Parts of the Constitution no longer in use or amended are crossed out ~~like this~~.

We the People of the United States, in Order to form a more perfect Union, establish Justice, insure domestic Tranquility, provide for the common defence, promote the general Welfare, and secure the Blessings of Liberty to ourselves and our Posterity, do ordain and establish this Constitution for the United States of America.

Article 1

Section 1—All legislative Powers herein granted shall be vested in a Congress of the United States, which shall consist of a Senate and House of Representatives.

Section 2—The House of Representatives shall be composed of Members chosen every second Year by the People of the several States, and the Electors in each State shall have the Qualifications requisite for Electors of the most numerous Branch of the State Legislature.

No person shall be a Representative who shall not have attained to the Age of twenty five Years, and been seven Years a Citizen of the United States, and who shall not, when elected, be an Inhabitant of that State in which he shall be chosen.

Representatives ~~and direct Taxes~~ shall be apportioned among the several States which may be included within this Union, according to their respective Numbers, ~~which shall be determined by adding to the whole Number of free Persons, including those bound to Service for a Term of Years, and excluding Indians not taxed, three fifths of all other Persons.~~ The actual Enumeration shall be made

Preamble (Introduction)

We, the people of the United States, have many goals. We want a better uniting of the states. We want fair laws. We want people to get along peacefully with one another. We want to be able to defend ourselves. We want a good life for everyone. We want the benefits of freedom for ourselves and for all future Americans. Therefore, we declare and set up this Constitution as the law of our land.

Article 1, Section 1.

The powers to make laws are given to the Congress of the United States. Congress has two parts. The two parts are called houses. One house is the Senate. The other is the House of Representatives.

Article 1, Section 2.

Clause 1. Each member of the House of Representatives has a two-year term. Members are elected by the people of each state. People who can vote for members of the larger house in their own state's lawmaking body can also vote for members of the House of Representatives.

Clause 2. To be representatives in the House, people must be (1) at least 25 years old, (2) citizens of the United States for at least 7 years, and (3) officially living in the state that elects them.

Clause 3. The number of representatives from a state depends on its population. In order to find out how many representatives a state had, the following steps were taken: (1) Count the number of free people. (2) Add three-fifths of "all other persons," that is, slaves. (3) Do not count American Indians who are not taxed. [Note: The 13th and 14th Amendments make the part of the

within three Years after the first Meeting of the Congress of the United States, and within every subsequent Term of ten Years, in such Manner as they shall by Law direct. The Number of Representatives shall not exceed one for every thirty Thousand, but each State shall have at Least one Representative: ~~and until such enumeration shall be made, the State of New Hampshire shall be entitled to chuse three, Massachusetts eight, Rhode Island and Providence Plantations one, Connecticut five, New York six, New Jersey four, Pennsylvania eight, Delaware one, Maryland six, Virginia ten, North Carolina five, South Carolina five, and Georgia three.~~

When vacancies happen in the Representation of any State, the Executive Authority thereof shall issue Writs of Election to fill such Vacancies.

The House of Representatives shall chuse their Speaker and other Officers; and shall have the sole Power of Impeachment.

Section 3—The Senate of the United States shall be composed of two Senators from each State, ~~chosen by the Legislature thereof,~~ for six Years; and each Senator shall have one Vote.

Immediately after they shall be assembled in Consequence of the first Election, they shall be divided as equally as may be into three Classes. The Seats of the Senators of the first Class shall be vacated at the Expiration of the second Year, of the second Class at the Expiration of the fourth Year, and of the third Class at the Expiration of the sixth Year, so that one third may be chosen every second

Constitution about slaves outdated. The part of the Constitution about direct taxes was changed by the 16th Amendment. By 1940, Native Americans were included in the counting.] A counting of the people shall be made. This was to happen within 3 years after the first meeting of the U.S. Congress. After that first meeting, a new counting shall take place every 10 years. Congress says how this census is to be done. There is not to be more than one representative for every 30,000 people. Each state must have at least one representative.

Clause 4. If a seat in the House becomes vacant, or empty, it must be filled. This can happen when a member of the House dies or leaves office. The governor of that member's state will set up a new election.

Clause 5. The members of the House of Representatives shall choose their Speaker (leader) and other officers. Only the members of the House have the power to impeach. To impeach is to bring charges against a high officer of the government for serious crimes. It is the first step in a process to remove such a person from power.

Article 1, Section 3.
Clause 1. The Senate is made up of two senators from each state. (Senators were chosen by the state legislatures.) [Note: This was changed in 1913 by the 17th Amendment. Now senators are elected directly by the people.] Every senator is elected for a 6-year term. Each senator has one vote.

Clause 2. One-third of the Senate is elected every two years. [Note: This has been the case except for the first Senate elected in 1789.] (The following was arranged so that we do not have all new senators every six years: Senators in the very first Congress were divided into three groups. One group left office after two years. The second left office after four years. The third group held

Year; and if Vacancies happen by Resignation, or otherwise, during the Recess of the Legislature of any State, the Executive thereof may make temporary Appointments until the next Meeting of the Legislature, which shall then fill such Vacancies.

No Person shall be a Senator who shall not have attained to the Age of thirty Years, and been nine Years a Citizen of the United States, and who shall not, when elected, be an Inhabitant of that State for which he shall be chosen.

The Vice President of the United States shall be President of the Senate, but shall have no Vote, unless they be equally divided.

The Senate shall chuse their other Officers, and also a President pro tempore, in the Absence of the Vice President, or when he shall exercise the Office of the President of the United States.

The Senate shall have the sole Power to try all Impeachments. When sitting for that Purpose, they shall be on Oath or Affirmation. When the President of the United States is tried, the Chief Justice shall preside: And no Person shall be convicted without the Concurrence of two thirds of the Members present.

Judgment in Cases of Impeachment shall not extend further than to removal from Office, and disqualification to hold and enjoy any Office of honor, Trust or Profit under the United States: but the Party convicted shall nevertheless be liable and subject to Indictment, Trial, Judgment and Punishment, according to Law.

Section 4—The Times, Places and Manner of holding Elections for Senators and Representatives, shall be prescribed in each State by the Legislature thereof; but the Congress may at any time by Law make or alter

office for the complete six-year term.)

If a senator resigns or dies, his or her seat in the Senate must be filled. (The old method of choosing a replacement was changed by the 17th Amendment in 1913.)

Clause 3. To be a senator, a person must be (1) at least 30 years old, (2) a U.S. citizen for at least 9 years, and (3) officially living in the state in which elected.

Clause 4. The vice-president of the United States is the leader or president of the Senate. He or she may vote at Senate meetings only when there is a tie.

Clause 5. The senators choose a member of the Senate to act as president pro tempore. He or she acts as the leader of the Senate when the vice-president of the United States is not in the Senate. The senators also choose nonmembers to act as Senate officials such as clerk and doorkeeper.

Clause 6. Only the Senate is allowed to decide if the person is guilty or not. The senators act as a jury. They are under oath. The chief justice of the Supreme Court runs the trial if the president of the United States is impeached. (In other cases, the vice-president runs the trial.) No one can be found guilty unless two-thirds of the senators present agree.

Clause 7. If a person is found guilty in an impeachment trial, he or she is punished by the Senate in two ways. One is by being removed from office. The second is by not being allowed ever again to hold a government job. If, however, the guilty person has broken a law, he or she may also have to go on trial before courts.

Article 1, Section 4.
Clause 1. Each state may decide the times, places, and ways of holding elections for the Senate and the House of Representatives. However, Congress can pass laws

such Regulations, except as to the Places of chusing Senators.

The Congress shall assemble at least once in every Year, and such Meeting shall ~~be on the first Monday in December,~~ unless they shall by Law appoint a different Day.

Section 5—Each House shall be the Judge of the Elections, Returns and Qualifications of its own Members, and a Majority of each shall constitute a Quorum to do Business; but a smaller Number may adjourn from day to day, and may be authorized to compel the Attendance of absent Members, in such Manner, and under such Penalties as each House may provide.

Each House may determine the Rules of its Proceedings, punish its Members for disorderly Behaviour, and, with the Concurrence of two thirds, expel a Member.

Each House shall keep a Journal of its Proceedings, and from time to time publish the same, excepting such Parts as may in their Judgment require Secrecy; and the Yeas and Nays of the Members of either House on any question shall, at the Desire of one fifth of those Present, be entered on the Journal.

Neither House, during the Session of Congress, shall, without the Consent of the other, adjourn for more than three days, nor to any other Place than that in which the two Houses shall be sitting.

Section 6—The Senators and Representatives shall receive a Compensation for their Services, to be ascertained by Law, and paid out of the Treasury of the United States. They shall in all Cases, except Treason, Felony and

that would change the state rules. But Congress may not change the places for choosing senators.

Clause 2. Congress must meet at least once a year. [Note: Congress no longer must meet on the first Monday in December. In 1933, the 20th Amendment changed the date to January 3.] Congress can change that date by law if it wants to.

Article 1, Section 5.
Clause 1. The House and the Senate may decide if new members are to be allowed in. They will check to see if people have been properly elected. They decide if someone is desirable as a member. The House and Senate cannot hold business meetings unless they have a quorum. This means that more than half the members must be present. Each house may make its own rules about making sure that members come to the meetings.

Clause 2. Each house is free to make its own rules. Each house may punish its members for not following the rules. Each house can remove a member from office if two-thirds of its members agree to do so.

Clause 3. Both the House and the Senate keep a journal. Each journal is a written record of what the house does and says. Both houses must print these records, and they must make them public. They may leave out what they decide needs to be kept secret. The way members voted on any question must be printed if one-fifth of the members present favor printing it.

Clause 4. Once Congress is in session neither house may stop meeting for more than three days. Any recess that lasts longer than that must be agreed upon by both houses. Both houses must always meet in the same place.

Article 1, Section 6.
Clause 1. Senators and representatives receive pay for their work. Laws are made to decide how much they will be paid. They are paid out of the United States Treasury.

Breach of the Peace, be privileged from Arrest during their Attendance at the Session of their respective Houses, and in going to and returning from the same; and for any Speech or Debate in either House, they shall not be questioned in any other Place.

No Senator or Representative shall, during the Time for which he was elected, be appointed to any civil Office under the Authority of the United States, which shall have been created, or the Emoluments whereof shall have been encreased during such time; and no Person holding any Office under the United States, shall be a Member of either House during his Continuance in Office.

Section 7—All Bills for raising Revenue shall originate in the House of Representatives; but the Senate may propose or concur with Amendments as on other Bills.

Every Bill which shall have passed the House of Representatives and the Senate, shall, before it become a Law, be presented to the President of the United States; If he approve he shall sign it, but if not he shall return it, with his Objections to that House in which it shall have originated, who shall enter the Objections at large on their Journal, and proceed to reconsider it. If after such Reconsideration two thirds of that House shall agree to pass the Bill, it shall be sent, together with the Objections, to the other House, by which it shall likewise be reconsidered, and if approved by two thirds of that House, it shall become a Law. But in all such Cases the Votes of both Houses shall be determined by yeas and Nays, and the Names of the Persons voting for and against the Bill shall be entered on the Journal of each House respectively. If any Bill shall not be returned by the President within ten Days (Sundays excepted) after it shall have been presented to him, the Same shall be a Law, in like Manner as if he had signed it, unless the Congress by their Adjournment prevent its Return, in which Case it shall not be a Law.

In most cases, while senators and representatives are meeting or going to and from meetings they are free from arrest. They can only be arrested for treason, for a felony, or for breaking the peace. No one may punish them for what they say in their meetings.

Clause 2. No senator or representative can take a newly created government job during the time for which he or she was elected. Members of Congress cannot leave office for another government job if the pay for that other job has been raised during their term in Congress. They also cannot hold any other government jobs while they are members of Congress.

Article 1, Section 7.
Clause 1. All bills for the raising of revenue must begin in the House of Representatives. The Senate may suggest changes in these tax bills.

Clause 2. To become a law, a bill must first pass both houses of Congress. The bill is then sent to the president of the United States. If the president approves of the bill, the president signs it. Then the bill becomes a law. If the president objects to the bill, the president can refuse to sign it. (This is called a veto.) The bill is then sent back to the house where it had started. When sending back a vetoed bill, the president tells why the bill was not signed.

The house that gets back the returned bill writes the president's objections (reasons for the veto) into its records. The members go over the bill again. If at least two-thirds of a house still votes for the bill, the bill is sent to the other house. The president's objections are also sent along. This house also goes over the bill again. If at least two-thirds of this house also votes for the bill, it becomes a law. The records of each house must show how each member voted. Yea votes are yes votes (that is, votes for the bill). Nay votes are no votes (votes against the bill). [Note: This two-thirds vote is one way a bill can become a law without the president's approval. This is called overriding the president's veto.] Congress overrides a veto when a two-thirds majority of each house passes the vetoed bill. After Congress sends a bill to the president, the president has 10 days (not counting Sundays) to act on a bill. If the president keeps it longer, the bill will become a law. [Note: This is a second way a bill can become a law without the president's signing it.] However, if Congress ends its session before the 10 days are up, the unsigned bill does not become law. (This is called a pocket veto. It is as if the president put the bill in a pocket and forgot it.)

Every Order, Resolution, or Vote to which the Concurrence of the Senate and House of Representatives may be necessary (except on a question of Adjournment) shall be presented to the President of the United States; and before the Same shall take Effect, shall be approved by him, or being disapproved by him, shall be repassed by two thirds of the Senate and House of Representatives, according to the Rules and Limitations prescribed in the Case of a Bill.

Clause 3. The president's approval is also needed for other actions in addition to the passing of laws. Any order, formal statement, or vote that is agreed to by both houses of Congress must be reported to the president. The president must then agree to It In order for the action to go into effect. If the president does not agree, Congress can follow the same rules as when the president does not sign a bill.

Congress does not need the president's approval to end its meeting for the year.

Section 8—The Congress shall have Power to lay and collect Taxes, Duties, Imposts and Excises, to pay the Debts and provide for the common Defence and general Welfare of the United States; but all Duties, Imposts and Excises shall be uniform throughout the United States;

Article 1, Section 8.
Clause 1. Congress has the power to tax. (It can decide what the taxes will be, and it can collect them.) The money raised may be used in three ways: (1) to pay what the government owes, (2) to defend the country, and (3) to pay for those services that would be good for the people. All federal taxes must be the same throughout the United States.

To borrow Money on the credit of the United States;

Clause 2. Congress has the power to borrow money with the promise to pay it back.

To regulate Commerce with foreign Nations, and among the several States, and with the Indian Tribes;

Clause 3. Congress has the power to make laws about trade. This is called the commerce clause. These rules can cover trade with other countries, trade among the states, and trade with Native American peoples.

To establish an uniform Rule of Naturalization, and uniform Laws on the subject of Bankruptcies throughout the United States;

Clause 4. Congress has the power to make one set of rules about how people can become United States citizens. Congress has the power to pass laws about people and businesses that are going broke. These laws must be the same for people in all the states.

To coin Money, regulate the Value thereof, and of foreign Coin, and fix the Standard of Weights and Measures;

Clause 5. Congress has the power to print and coin money and to say how much it is worth. It can say how much foreign money is worth in American money, and how things should be weighed and measured.

To provide for the Punishment of counterfeiting the Securities and current Coin of the United States;

Clause 6. Congress has the power to punish people who make fake United States bonds or money.

To establish Post Offices and post Roads;

Clause 7. Congress has the power to set up post offices. It can also set up post roads. (These are roads to be used in delivering mail.)

To promote the Progress of Science and useful Arts, by securing for limited Times to Authors and Inventors the exclusive Rights to their respective Writings and Discoveries;

Clause 8. Congress has the power to help the growth of science, the arts, and learning. It can pass laws giving patents to inventors and copyrights to authors. (These laws protect their work from being stolen or copied without permission for a certain time.)

To constitute Tribunals inferior to the supreme Court;

Clause 9. Congress has the power to set up courts, which must be less powerful than the Supreme Court.

To define and punish Piracies and Felonies committed on the high Seas, and Offences against the Law of Nations;

Clause 10. Congress has the power to name those actions that are thought to be crimes on the high seas. It has the power to punish people who break laws that nations have agreed upon (international law).

To declare War, grant Letters of Marque and Reprisal, and make Rules concerning Captures on Land and Water;

Clause 11. Congress has the power to declare war. (However, Congress no longer gives special "letters"—licenses—to privately owned armed ships. These letters allowed private ships to attack enemy ships during wartime.) Congress has the power to make rules about taking enemy property on land or sea.

To raise and support Armies, but no Appropriation of Money to that Use shall be for a longer Term than two Years;

Clause 12. Congress has the power to set up and supply armies. It cannot provide monies for the army for more than two years at a time.

To provide and maintain a Navy;

Clause 13. Congress has the power to set up and supply a navy.

To make Rules for the Government and Regulation of the land and naval Forces;

Clause 14. Congress has the power to make rules to keep order in the army and navy.

To provide for calling forth the Militia to execute the Laws of the Union, suppress Insurrections and repel Invasions;

Clause 15. Congress can call for help from a state's militia for any of three reasons. (1) One reason is to uphold the nation's laws. (2) A second reason is to fight people who wish to overthrow the government. (3) A third reason is to fight people who attack the country.

To provide for organizing, arming, and disciplining, the Militia, and for governing such Part of them as may be employed in the Service of the United States, reserving to the States respectively, the Appointment of the Officers, and the Authority of training the Militia according to the discipline prescribed by Congress;

Clause 16. Congress has the power to make rules for forming, arming, and keeping order In state militias. Congress can also make rules about how these soldiers shall serve the country. The states have the right to pick the officers for the militia. States must train the militia according to the rules made by Congress.

To exercise exclusive Legislation in all Cases whatsoever, over such District (not exceeding ten Miles square) as may, by Cession of particular States, and the Acceptance of Congress, become the Seat of the Government of the United States, and to exercise like Authority over all Places purchased by the Consent of the Legislature of the State in which the Same shall be, for the Erection of Forts, Magazines, Arsenals, dock-Yards, and other needful Buildings;—And

Clause 17. Congress has the power to make all laws for the place where it will meet. This place is to be in a spot no bigger than 10 miles square. [Note: This place is now Washington, District of Columbia.] Congress rules over all places that it buys from the states. These places may be used for forts or for the storing of weapons. They may be used for navy yards and for other buildings as needed.

To make all Laws which shall be necessary and proper for carrying into Execution the foregoing Powers, and all other Powers vested by this Constitution in the Government of the United States, or in any Department or Officer thereof.

Clause 18. Congress has the power to make any laws it may need to use the powers listed in the above 17 clauses. Laws needed to carry out other powers given by the Constitution shall also be made by Congress.

Section 9—~~The Migration or Importation of such Persons as any of the States now existing shall think proper to admit, shall not be pro-~~

Article 1, Section 9.
Clause 1. Congress did not have the power to stop the areas that were states in 1788

hibited by the Congress prior to the Year one thousand eight hundred and eight, but a Tax or duty may be imposed on such Importation, not exceedig ten dollars for each Person.

from bringing in as many slaves ("such Persons") as they wanted until the year 1808. Congress could place a tax up to $10 on each slave brought into the country. In 1808 it became illegal to import slaves.

The Privilege of the Writ of Habeas Corpus shall not be suspended, unless when in Cases of Rebellion or Invasion the public Safety may require it.

Clause 2. Only in cases of rebellion, where people use open, armed force to try to overthrow the government, or invasion can the writ of habeas corpus be taken away. Therefore, prisoners must be either freed or brought into court. In the court, a judge will tell them the reason why they are being held. The judge will also decide if a prisoner is being held lawfully.

No Bill of Attainder or ex post facto Law shall be passed.

Clause 3. Congress is not allowed to pass a law that, without a trial, finds a person guilty of treason or other serious crime. Also, Congress is not allowed to pass laws that punish people for doing something that had not been against the law when they did it.

No Capitation, or other direct, Tax shall be laid, unless in Proportion to the Census or Enumeration herein before directed to be taken.

Clause 4. No persons in the United States may be taxed unless everyone is taxed in the same way. Congress must base taxes on population. [Note: This was changed in part by the 16th Amendment, which made an income tax legal. The 24th Amendment outlaws the tax that used to be placed on those who voted.]

No Tax or Duty shall be laid on Articles exported from any State.

Clause 5. Congress does not have the power to put a tax on goods being sent out of any state.

No Preference shall be given by any Regulation of Commerce or Revenue to the Ports of one State over those of another: nor shall Vessels bound to, or from, one State, be obliged to enter, clear, or pay Duties in another.

Clause 6. Congress does not have the power to make trade laws that would favor one state over another. Ships going from one state to another may not be taxed.

No Money shall be drawn from the Treasury, but in Consequence of Appropriations made by Law; and a regular Statement and Account of the Receipts and Expenditures of all public Money shall be published from time to time.

Clause 7. No government money can be spent unless Congress passes a law giving its permission. A record of how much money has been collected and spent must be kept, and this information must also be made public.

No Title of Nobility shall be granted by the United States: And no Person holding any Office of Profit or Trust under them, shall, without the Consent of the Congress, accept of any present, Emolument, Office, or Title, of any kind whatever, from any King, Prince, or foreign State.

Section 10—No State shall enter into any Treaty, Alliance, or Confederation; grant Letters of Marque and Reprisal; coin Money; emit Bills of Credit; make any Thing but gold and silver Coin a Tender in Payment of Debts; pass any Bill of Attainder, ex post facto Law, or Law impairing the Obligation of Contracts, or grant any Title of Nobility.

No State shall, without the Consent of the Congress, lay any Imposts or Duties on Imports or Exports, except what may be absolutely necessary for executing its inspection Laws: and the net Produce of all Duties and Imposts, laid by any State on Imports or Exports, shall be for the Use of the Treasury of the United States; and all such Laws shall be subject to the Revision and Controul of the Congress.

No State shall, without the Consent of Congress, lay any Duty of Tonnage, keep Troops, or Ships of War in time of Peace, enter into any Agreement or Compact with another State, or with a foreign Power, or engage in War, unless actually invaded, or in such imminent Danger as will not admit of delay.

Article II
Section 1—The executive Power shall be vested in a President of the United States of

Clause 8. No titles of nobility (such as *king, duke, baron,* or *earl*) may be given to anyone by the government. No government worker may accept a gift, title, or job from a foreign country unless Congress agrees.

Article 1, Section 10.
Clause 1. No state is allowed to make a treaty with any country. No state can become part of another country. No state can give its citizens the right to fight other countries. No state can make coin or paper money. No state can pass a law that allows anything but gold and silver to be used as money. No state may allow a person to be punished for doing something without a fair trial. Nor may a person be punished for doing something that was not against the law when it was done. No state can pass a law that would excuse a person, business, or group from a contract. No state can give anyone a title of nobility.

Clause 2. Unless Congress agrees, no state may put a tax on goods entering or leaving the state. However, an inspection fee may be charged if necessary. Congress may allow taxes on goods entering or leaving the state. All money made from these taxes shall go to the national government (the U.S. Treasury). Congress may change any of these kinds of tax laws.

Clause 3. Unless Congress agrees, no state can do any of the following: No state may tax ships. No state may keep warships or have troops in times of peace (except for the militia). No state may make deals with other states or with foreign countries. No state can go to war unless it is attacked or is in such great danger that it cannot put off fighting.

Article 2, Section 1.
Clause 1. The power to make people follow the laws is given to the president of

America. He shall hold his Office during the Term of four Years, and, together with the Vice President, chosen for the same Term, be elected, as follows

Each State shall appoint, in such Manner as the Legislature thereof may direct, a Number of Electors, equal to the whole Number of Senators and Representatives to which the State may be entitled in the Congress: but no Senator or Representative, or Person holding an Office of Trust or Profit under the United States, shall be appointed an Elector.

~~The Electors shall meet in their respective States, and vote by Ballot for two Persons, of whom one at least shall not be an inhabitant of the same State with themselves. And they shall make a List of all the Persons voted for, and of the Number of Votes for each; which List they shall sign and certify, and transmit sealed to the Seat of the Government of the United States, directed to the President of the Senate. The President of the Senate shall, in the Presence of the Senate and House of Representatives, open all the Certificates, and the Votes shall then be counted. The Person having the greatest Number of Votes shall be the President, if such Number be a Majority of the whole Number of Electors appointed; and if there be more than one who have such Majority, and have an equal Number of Votes, then the House of Representatives shall immediately chuse by Ballot one of them for President; and if no Person have a Majority, then from the five highest on the List the said House shall in like Manner chuse the President. But in chusing the President, the Votes shall be taken by States, the Representation from each State having one Vote; A quorum for this Purpose shall consist of a Member or Members from two thirds of the States, and a Majority of all the States shall be necessary to a Choice. In every Case, after the Choice of the President, the Person having the greatest Number of Votes of the Electors shall be the Vice President. But if there should remain two or more who have equal Votes, the Senate shall chuse from them by Ballot the Vice President.~~

the United States of America. The president's term of office is four years. The vice-president has the same term. Both are elected as follows:

Clause 2. Each state's legislature decides how to choose its electors. Each state gets electors equal to the number of people it has in Congress. No senator or representative may be an elector. No one who holds an office in the national government may be an elector.

Clause 3. [Note: The 12th Amendment has made changes in the way the president is elected. The following describes the old way.] The electors made up the electoral college. They each voted for two people, at least one being from another state. They met in their own states. In each state the votes were counted. The list of people voted for was then sealed. The lists were sent to the president of the Senate. All the lists were opened by the president of the Senate. The votes were then counted before both houses of Congress. The person with the most electoral votes and a majority of the electoral votes became president. The person with the next highest electoral vote total became vice-president. But there could be a tie with both people also having a majority of the electors' votes. Then the House of Representatives voted to make one of them president.

What if the counting of the votes from the states' lists showed that no one had a majority of electors' votes? Then the House of Representatives chose for president from among the top five vote getters. In such cases, each state had only one vote in the House of Representatives. The winner had to get a majority of the votes cast in the House. The winner became the president. After the president was chosen, the person with the next highest number of votes of electors became vice-president. If there was a tie, the Senate voted for the vice-president from among the people who were involved in the tie.

The Congress may determine the Time of chusing the Electors, and the Day on which they shall give their Votes; which Day shall be the same throughout the United States.

Clause 4. Congress sets the time for the election for president. That is the time when the electors are chosen. Congress also sets the day the electors vote. Everywhere in the United States people have the same voting day. [Note: Congress has set the election for president every four years on the Tuesday following the first Monday in November. The electors vote on the Monday after the second Wednesday in December.]

No Person except a natural born Citizen, or a Citizen of the United States, at the time of the Adoption of this Constitution, shall be eligible to the Office of President; neither shall any Person be eligible to that Office who shall not have attained to the Age of thirty five Years, and been fourteen Years a Resident within the United States.

Clause 5. To become president, a person must have been born a citizen of the United States. (The Constitution had a rule to allow a person to become president even if not born a U.S. citizen. That could happen only if the person was a U.S. citizen when the Constitution was adopted.) This person must be at least 35 years old. The person must also have lived in the United States for at least 14 years.

In Case of the Removal of the President from Office, or of his Death, Resignation, or Inability to discharge the Powers and Duties of the said Office, the Same shall devolve on the Vice President, and the Congress may by Law provide for the Case of Removal, Death, Resignation or Inability, both of the President and Vice President, declaring what Officer shall then act as President, and such Officer shall act accordingly, until the Disability be removed, or a President shall be elected.

Clause 6. If the president is removed from office, dies, quits the job, or becomes very sick, the vice-president becomes president. [Note: The president can be removed from office by being found guilty in an impeachment trial.] Congress can make the rules in cases where no vice-president is available. [Note: This is the original way in which the office was filled. This section was changed by the 25th Amendment in 1967.]

The President shall, at stated Times, receive for his Services, a Compensation, which shall neither be encreased nor diminished during the Period for which he shall have been elected, and he shall not receive within that Period any other Emolument from the United States, or any of them.

Clause 7. While in office, the president gets paid for doing the job. While in office, the president's salary cannot be changed. The president cannot be given any other payment by a state or the national government while in office.

Before he enter on the Execution of his Office, he shall take the following Oath or Affirmation:—"I do solemnly swear (or affirm) that I will faithfully execute the Office of President of the United States, and will to the best of my Ability, preserve, protect and defend the Constitution of the United States."

Clause 8. Before taking office, the person who will become president must take an oath of office. The president promises to carry out faithfully the duties of the job. The president promises to uphold, protect, and defend the Constitution.

Section 2—The President shall be Commander in Chief of the Army and Navy of the United States, and of the Militia of the several States, when called into the actual Service of the United States; he may require the Opinion, in writing, of the principal Officer in each of the executive Departments, upon any Subject relating to the Duties of their respective Offices, and he shall have Power to grant Reprieves and Pardons for Offences against the United States, except in Cases of Impeachment.

He shall have Power, by and with the Advice and Consent of the Senate, to make Treaties, provided two thirds of the Senators present concur; and he shall nominate, and by and with the Advice and Consent of the Senate, shall appoint Ambassadors, other public Ministers and Consuls, Judges of the supreme Court, and all other Officers of the United States, whose Appointments are not herein otherwise provided for, and which shall be established by Law: but the Congress may by Law vest the Appointment of such inferior Officers, as they think proper, in the President alone, in the Courts of Law, or in the Heads of Departments.

The President shall have Power to fill up all Vacancies that may happen during the Recess of the Senate, by granting Commissions which shall expire at the End of their next Session.

Section 3—He shall from time to time give to the Congress Information of the State of the Union, and recommend to their Consideration such Measures as he shall judge necessary and expedient; he may, on extraordinary Occasions, convene both Houses, or either of them, and in Case of Disagreement between them, with Respect to the Time of Adjournment, he may adjourn them to such Time as he shall think proper; he shall receive Ambassadors and other public Ministers; he shall

Article 2, Section 2.
Clause 1. The president is commander in chief of the country's military (armed forces). This includes the state militias (National Guard) when the country needs them. When asked, each of the heads of executive departments has to report to the president about the work his or her department does. The president has the right to delay a person's punishment for a federal crime. The president can pardon a person found guilty of a federal crime, but the president cannot delay a punishment or give a pardon in cases of impeachment.

Clause 2. The president has the power to make treaties with other nations. The treaty does not go into effect unless two-thirds of the senators present at a meeting of the Senate approve it. The president appoints people to represent the United States in other countries. The president appoints judges to the Supreme Court. The president also appoints other national officials whose jobs the Constitution does not mention. Each appointment must be approved by a majority of the Senate. The president may appoint less important officials without Senate approval. But that can be done only when the laws of Congress allow it. If the laws allow it, the courts and heads of government departments also may appoint less important officials.

Clause 3. When Congress is not meeting, the president may appoint people to unfilled government jobs. These people may hold the jobs until the end of the next meeting of the Senate.

Article 2, Section 3.
From time to time the president will address Congress about the condition of the country. When necessary, the president will suggest actions for Congress to take. This is called the State of the Union Address. In an emergency or for special reasons, the president may call either house, or both houses, together for a special meeting. If Congress cannot decide when to stop meeting, the president may tell them

take Care that the Laws be faithfully executed, and shall Commission all the Officers of the United States.

Section 4—The President, Vice President and all civil Officers of the United States, shall be removed from Office on Impeachment for, and Conviction of, Treason, Bribery, or other high Crimes and Misdemeanors.

Article III
Section 1—The judicial Power of the United States, shall be vested in one supreme Court, and in such inferior Courts as the Congress may from time to time ordain and establish. The Judges, both of the supreme and inferior Courts, shall hold their Offices during good Behaviour, and shall, at stated Times, receive for their Services, a Compensation, which shall not be diminished during their Continuance in Office.

Section 2—The judicial Power shall extend to all Cases, in Law and Equity, arising under this Constitution, the Laws of the United States, and Treaties made, or which shall be made, under their Authority;—to all Cases affecting Ambassadors, other public Ministers and Consuls;—to all Cases of admiralty and maritime Jurisdiction;—to Controversies to which the United States shall be a Party;—to Controversies between two or more States;—between a State and Citizens of another State;—between Citizens of different States,—between Citizens of the same State claiming Lands under Grants of different

when to stop. The president shall greet government officials from other countries. [Note: The power to greet such people is the power to deal with other nations.] The president is to see that the nation's laws are followed. The president signs the papers that give government officials the right to do their jobs.

Article 2, Section 4.
There is a way to remove the president, vice-president, and all other civil officers from their jobs. They may be removed from office for certain crimes through impeachment and conviction for certain crimes. They may be removed from office for three reasons. One is giving help to the country's enemies, or helping them fight against this country. Another reason is illegally taking money or other items of value to influence the actions, votes, or opinions of people in any public office or official capacity. The third is carrying out other serious crimes.

Article 3, Section 1.
Judicial power is given to the Supreme Court. It is also given to lower federal courts that Congress wants to set up. The judges in these courts keep their jobs for life. However, they can be removed from office if they are found to have done something really wrong. (They must be impeached and convicted before they can be removed from office.) They are to be paid for their work, and this pay cannot be made less while they keep their jobs.

Article 3, Section 2.
Clause 1. The federal courts have the right to try many kinds of cases. The federal courts can rule on all cases having to do with the Constitution and the laws of the United States. They can try cases dealing with treaties made by the United States. They can settle cases involving other governments' representatives in the United States. They can try cases having to do with shipping or ships. Federal courts can hear cases in which the United States is a party. They can hear cases between two or more states. [Note: Federal courts used to

States, and between a State, or the Citizens thereof, and foreign States, Citizens or Subjects.

hear cases between a state and people of another state. This was changed by the 11th Amendment in 1798.] The federal courts hear cases between people of different states. They hear cases where people from the same state both claim to own land in another state. They also hear cases of states or Americans versus other countries or the people of other countries.

In all Cases affecting Ambassadors, other public Ministers and Consuls, and those in which a State shall be Party, the supreme Court shall have original Jurisdiction. In all the other Cases before mentioned, the supreme Court shall have appellate Jurisdiction, both as to Law and Fact, with such Exceptions, and under such Regulations as the Congress shall make.

Clause 2. The Supreme Court has two types of jurisdiction. (1) It can hear a case for the first time if the case involves a representative of another country or if one of the states is in the case. All other kinds of cases are tried in the lower courts first. (2) The Supreme Court can hear a case on appeal from a lower court. This means it can review the ruling of the lower court. Congress decides what kinds of rules apply to cases that may be appealed.

The Trial of all Crimes, except in Cases of Impeachment, shall be by Jury; and such Trial shall be held in the State where the said Crimes shall have been committed; but when not committed within any State, the Trial shall be at such Place or Places as the Congress may by Law have directed.

Clause 3. Cases of impeachment are not tried by a jury. Cases dealing with crimes that can be tried in the federal courts must be trials by jury. The trial should be held in the state where the federal law was broken. If the crime took place outside of a state (such as on a ship at sea), Congress will say where the trial will be held.

Section 3—Treason against the United States, shall consist only in levying War against them, or in adhering to their Enemies, giving them Aid and Comfort. No Person shall be convicted of Treason unless on the Testimony of two Witnesses to the same overt Act, or on Confession in open Court.

Article 3, Section 3.
Clause 1. Treason against the United States can mean a person has done one or both of the following actions. Treason can mean making war against his or her country. Treason can mean giving help to one's country's enemies.

As part of convicting a person of treason one of two things must be done. One is for at least two witnesses to say in court that they saw the accused person do the same act of treason. The other is for the person who is on trial to admit being guilty in open court.

The Congress shall have Power to declare the Punishment of Treason, but no Attainder of Treason shall work Corruption

Clause 2. Congress has the power to pass laws about how treason is punished. Only the guilty person can be punished. That

of Blood, or Forfeiture except during the Life of the Person attainted.

Article IV

Section 1—Full Faith and Credit shall be given in each State to the public Acts, Records, and judicial Proceedings of every other State. And the Congress may by general Laws prescribe the Manner in which such Acts, Records and Proceedings shall be proved, and the Effect thereof.

Section 2—The Citizens of each State shall be entitled to all Privileges and Immunities of Citizens in the several States.

A Person charged in any State with Treason, Felony, or other Crime, who shall flee from Justice, and be found in another State, shall on Demand of the executive Authority of the State from which he fled, be delivered up, to be removed to the State having Jurisdiction of the Crime.

~~No Person held to Service or Labour in one State, under the Laws thereof, escaping into another, shall, in Consequence of any Law or Regulation therein, be discharged from such Service or Labour, but shall be delivered up on Claim of the Party to whom such Service or Labour may be due.~~

Section 3—New States may be admitted by the Congress into this Union; but no new State shall be formed or erected within the Jurisdiction of any other State; nor any State be formed by the Junction of two or more States, or Parts of States, without the Consent of the Legislatures of the States concerned as well as of the Congress.

The Congress shall have Power to dispose of and make all needful Rules and Regulations respecting the Territory or other Property belonging to the United States; and nothing in this Constitution shall be so construed as to Prejudice any Claims of the United States, or of any particular State.

person's family and children cannot be punished because of the treason.

Article 4, Section 1.

Each state must respect the laws, records, and court decisions of all the other states. Congress has the power to say how this works among the states.

Article 4, Section 2.

Clause 1. A citizen of one state has the same rights when visiting or dealing with another state as the citizens of every state.

Clause 2. This is the rule about people who are charged with a crime in one state and who run away from trial or legal punishment to another state. The governor of the state where the crime happened can ask to have the accused person sent back for a trial. The state to which the person moved is supposed to return the person for trial.

Clause 3. No one who was a slave in one state could be made free by running away to another state. This was changed by the 13th Amendment in 1865.

Article 4, Section 3.

Clause 1. The power to add new states to the Union is given to Congress. No new state can be formed from part of another state unless that older state allows it. A new state cannot be formed from parts of two or more older states unless the legislatures of those older states and Congress both allow it.

Clause 2. Congress can sell or give away any land or property belonging to the United States. Congress may make laws or rules for U.S. territories or other property. Nothing in the Constitution is to favor one state over another or the United States over any state when there are arguments about land claims.

Section 4—The United States shall guarantee to every State in this Union a Republican Form of Government, and shall protect each of them against Invasion; and on Application of the Legislature, or of the Executive (when the Legislature cannot be convened) against domestic Violence.

Article 4, Section 4.
The federal government promises that each state will have a republican government. It promises to protect the states from enemies entering the states by force. If fights (riots) break out within any state, the United States government promises help. It will help when the state's legislature or governor asks it to help.

Article V
The Congress, whenever two thirds of both Houses shall deem it necessary, shall propose Amendments to this Constitution, or, on the Application of the Legislatures of two thirds of the several States, shall call a Convention for proposing Amendments, which, in either Case, shall be valid to all Intents and Purposes, as Part of this Constitution, when ratified by the Legislatures of three fourths of the several States, or by Conventions in three fourths thereof, as the one or the other Mode of Ratification may be proposed by the Congress; Provided ~~that no Amendment which may be made prior to the Year One thousand eight hundred and eight shall in any Manner affect the first and fourth Clauses in the Ninth Section of the first Article; and~~ that no State, without its Consent, shall be deprived of its equal Suffrage in the Senate.

Article 5
There are two steps to amending the Constitution. The first step is proposing, or suggesting, the change. This can be done in two ways. (1) Two-thirds of each house of Congress can vote for the change. (2) Two-thirds of the states' legislatures can ask Congress to call a national convention to suggest the amendment.

The second step is ratifying, or approving, the change or amendment. All amendments must be agreed to by the states. This can be done in two ways. (1) Three-fourths of the states' legislatures can ratify the amendment. (2) Each state can hold a special convention about the proposed change. The amendment is ratified if three-fourths of these state conventions approve it. Congress has the power to say which of the two ways the amendment is to be ratified. (Part of this article said no amendments before 1808 could deal with the slave trade. That part is no longer in effect.) No amendment can make any state have fewer senators in the Senate than other states unless the state agrees to the change.

Article VI
All Debts contracted and Engagements entered into, before the Adoption of this Constitution, shall be as valid against the United States under this Constitution, as under the Confederation.

This Constitution, and the Laws of the United States which shall be made in Pursuance thereof; and all Treaties made, or which shall be made, under the Authority of the United States, shall be the supreme Law of

Article 6
Clause 1. The government agreed to accept all past debts and treaties made under the Articles of Confederation.

Clause 2. This Constitution, the laws made by Congress, and all treaties by the United States are the most powerful in the land. State judges must follow these laws even if state laws do not agree with them.

the Land; and the Judges in every State shall be bound thereby, any Thing in the Constitution or Laws of any State to the Contrary notwithstanding.

The Senators and Representatives before mentioned, and the Members of the several State Legislatures, and all executive and judicial Officers, both of the United States and of the several States, shall be bound by Oath or Affirmation, to support this Constitution; but no religious Test shall ever be required as a Qualification to any Office or public Trust under the United States.

Clause 3. Federal and state officials must promise to obey the U.S. Constitution. No one may be kept out of a government job because of his or her religion.

Article VII
The Ratification of the Conventions of nine States, shall be sufficient of the Establishment of this Constitution between the States so ratifying the Same.

Done in Convention by the Unanimous Consent of the States present the Seventeenth Day of September in the Year of our Lord one thousand seven hundred and Eighty seven and of the Independence of the United States of America the Twelfth IN WITNESS whereof We have hereunto subscribed our Names,

Article 7
This Constitution will be set up for the approving states when 9 of the 13 states have approved it. Each state will vote to approve it in its own special convention.

It is being signed on September 17, 1787, when the country is almost 12 years old. The people who are signing are from all the states represented at the Constitutional Convention on that day. Here are the names:

G^R WASHINGTON—
Presid. and deputy from Virginia

New Hampshire
John Langdon
Nicholas Gilman

Massachusetts
Nathaniel Gorham
Rufus King

Connecticut
Wm. Saml. Johnson
Roger Sherman

New York
Alexander Hamilton

New Jersey
Wil: Livingston
David Brearley
Wm. Paterson
Jona: Dayton

Pennsylvania
B Franklin
Thomas Mifflin
Robt Morris
Geo. Clymer
Thos. FitzSimons
Jared Ingersoll
James Wilson
Gouv Morris

Delaware
Geo: Read
Gunning Bedford jun
John Dickinson
Richard Bassett
Jaco: Broom

Maryland
James McHenry
Dan of St Thos. Jenifer
Danl Carroll

Virginia
John Blair—
James Madison Jr.

North Carolina
Wm. Blount
Rich'd Dobbs Spaight
Hu Williamson

South Carolina
J. Rutledge
Charles Cotesworth Pinckney
Charles Pinckney
Pierce Butler

Georgia
William Few
Abr Baldwin

Attest:
William Jackson, *Secretary*

[Note that each of the following 26 amendments to the original Constitution is called an "Article." Only the 13th, 14th, 15th, and 16th Amendments had actual numbers at the time of their ratification. The first 10 amendments are called the Bill of Rights.]

Article

Congress shall make no law respecting an establishment of religion, or prohibiting the free exercise thereof; or abridging the freedom of speech, or of the press; or the right of the people peaceably to assemble, and to petition the Government for a redress of grievances.

Amendment 1 (1791)

Congress cannot pass any laws setting up an official religion. It cannot pass laws to stop people from freely following their religion.

Congress cannot make laws keeping people from saying what they want. [Note: Laws may punish people for speaking or printing things that limit the rights of others.]

Congress cannot make laws keeping people from printing what they think.

Congress cannot make laws that keep people from meeting peacefully.

Congress cannot keep people from petitioning the government. That means the right of asking the government to correct what they feel is wrong.

Article

A well regulated Militia, being necessary to the security of a free State, the right of the people to keep and bear Arms, shall not be infringed.

Amendment 2 (1791)

A strong state militia is needed for the security of the state. Congress cannot go against the people's right to keep and carry guns.

Article

No Soldier shall, in time of peace be quartered in any house, without the consent of the Owner, nor in time of war, but in a manner to be prescribed by law.

Amendment 3 (1791)

In peacetime, no one has to give soldiers a place to sleep or meals in his or her home. In wartime, this can happen only if Congress says so with a law.

Article

The right of the people to be secure in their persons, houses, papers, and effects, against unreasonable searches and seizures, shall not be violated, and no Warrants shall issue, but upon probable cause, supported by Oath or affirmation, and particularly describing the place to be searched, and the persons or things to be seized.

Amendment 4 (1791)

The people, their homes, their papers, and their property are safe from unreasonable searches. A person and the things he or she owns cannot be taken away except in ways that follow the law. Before seizing evidence or people, a search warrant or arrest warrant must be given by a court. However, it can be given only for good reasons. Persons who want a search warrant must promise they are telling the truth. They must explain why they want the warrant. If they plan to search, they must say beforehand what place is to be searched. If they plan to take someone or something away, they must say beforehand what person or things are to be taken.

Article

No person shall be held to answer for a capital, or otherwise infamous crime, unless on a presentment or indictment of a Grand Jury, except in cases arising in the land or naval forces, or in the Militia, when in actual service in time of War or public danger; nor shall any person be subject for the same offence to be twice put in jeopardy of life or limb; nor shall be compelled in any criminal case to be a witness against himself, nor be deprived of life, liberty, or property, without due process of law; nor shall private property be taken for public use without just compensation.

Article

In all criminal prosecutions, the accused shall enjoy the right to a speedy and public trial, by an impartial jury of the State and district wherein the crime shall have been committed, which district shall have been previously ascertained by law, and to be informed of the nature and cause of the accusation; to be confronted with the witnesses against him; to have compulsory process for obtaining Witnesses in his favor, and to have the assistance of counsel for his defence.

Article

In Suits at common law, where the value in controversy shall exceed twenty dollars, the right of trial by jury shall be preserved, and no fact tried by a jury, shall be otherwise reexamined in any Court of the United States, than according to the rules of the common law.

Article

Excessive bail shall not be required, nor excessive fines imposed, nor cruel and unusual punishments inflicted.

Amendment 5 (1791)

A person must be accused by a grand jury before being put on trial for a crime that can be punished by death or for any other serious crime. This rule does not hold true for members of the armed forces in times of war or danger to the country.

No person may be tried twice for the same crime. Accused persons cannot be forced to give evidence against themselves in criminal cases.

Accused people should not lose their lives, liberty, or property except by due process of law. If the government takes private property for public use, it must pay a fair price for it.

Amendment 6 (1791)

A person accused of a crime has the right to a speedy trial. It must be a public trial. There must be a fair jury. The trial should be held in the state and district where the crime took place. The accused person must be told what he or she is being tried for. The accused person has the right to see, hear, and question witnesses against him or her in the courtroom. The accused person may know of and want witnesses to speak in his or her favor. If so, the court must bring these witnesses to give evidence at the trial. An accused person has the right to have a lawyer defend him or her.

Amendment 7 (1791)

People have a right to a jury trial if the case involves more than $20.

A ruling of a jury cannot be changed except in two ways. One way happens when there is a new trial with another jury. The second way happens if a higher court takes the case because there was a mistake made in the law.

Amendment 8 (1791)

Accused persons cannot be asked to pay more bail than is fair for the crime done. People cannot be asked to pay fines that are too high and therefore unfair for the crime done. People cannot be punished in cruel and unusual ways.

Article

The enumeration in the Constitution, of certain rights, shall not be construed to deny or disparage others retained by the people.

Article

The powers not delegated to the United States by the Constitution, nor prohibited by it to the States, are reserved to the States respectively, or to the people.

Article

The Judicial power of the United States shall not be construed to extend to any suit in law or equity, commenced or prosecuted against one of the United States by Citizens of another State, or by Citizens or Subjects of any Foreign State.

Article

The electors shall meet in their respective states and vote by ballot for President and Vice-President, one of whom, at least, shall not be an inhabitant of the same state with themselves; they shall name in their ballots the person voted for as President, and in distinct ballots the person voted for as Vice-President, and they shall make distinct lists of all persons voted for as President, and of all persons voted for as Vice-President, and of the number of votes for each, which lists they shall sign and certify, and transmit sealed to the seat of the government of the United States, directed to the President of the Senate;

—The President of the Senate shall, in the presence of the Senate and House of Representatives, open all the certificates and the votes shall then be counted;

—The person having the greatest number of votes for President, shall be the President, if such number be a majority of the whole number of Electors appointed; and if no person have such majority, then from the persons having the highest numbers not exceeding three on the list of those voted for as President, the House of Representatives shall choose immediately, by ballot, the President.

Amendment 9 (1791)

The Constitution lists certain rights. If other rights are not listed, that does not mean people do not have those rights.

Amendment 10 (1791)

All powers not given to the United States by the Constitution, nor forbidden by it to the states, belong to the states or to the people.

Amendment 11 (1798)

A case may not be brought against a state in a federal court by persons of another state or persons of another nation.

Amendment 12 (1804)

The electors meet in their own states. They vote by marking two ballots. One is for president. The other is for vice-president. At least one of the candidates an elector votes for must live in some other state than the state the elector lives in. After the vote, the electors make two lists. One is a list of all the persons the electors voted for as president. The other is a list of all the persons the electors voted for as vice-president. On each list they write the number of electoral votes each person got. Then they sign their names and seal the lists. They send the lists to the president of the Senate in Washington, D.C.

The president of the Senate opens the lists in front of the members of both houses. The votes are then counted.

The person having the most votes for president becomes the president. However, that person must have more than half of all the electoral votes. If no person has over half the votes, the House of Representatives must choose the president. The House chooses from the three people on the list who have the most electoral votes. Each state has only one vote, no matter

But in choosing the President, the votes shall be taken by states, the representation from each state having one vote; a quorum for this purpose shall consist of a member or members from two-thirds of the states, and a majority of all the states shall be necessary to a choice.

~~And if the House of Representatives shall not choose a President whenever the right of choice shall devolve upon them, before the fourth day of March next following, then the Vice-President shall act as President, as in the case of the death or other constitutional disability of the President.~~

The person having the greatest number of votes as Vice-President, shall be the Vice-President, if such number be a majority of the whole number of Electors appointed, and if no person have a majority, then from the two highest numbers on the list, the Senate shall choose the Vice-President; a quorum for the purpose shall consist of two-thirds of the whole number of Senators, and a majority of the whole number shall be necessary to a choice.

But no person constitutionally ineligible to the office of President shall be eligible to that of Vice-President of the United States.

Article XIII
Section 1—Neither slavery nor involuntary servitude, except as a punishment for crime whereof the party shall have been duly convicted, shall exist within the United States, or any place subject to their jurisdiction.

Section 2—Congress shall have power to enforce this article by appropriate legislation.

Article XIV
Section 1—All persons born or naturalized in the United States, and subject to the jurisdiction thereof, are citizens of the United States and of the State wherein they reside. No State

how many representatives it has. At least two-thirds of the states must vote. To be elected president, a person needs more than half the votes of all the states.

The House must try to elect a president before the date set for the new president to take office. [Note: This date was changed to January 20 by the 20th Amendment.] If the House cannot, then the vice-president shall act as president.

The person who has the most votes for vice-president becomes vice-president. However, that person must have over half of all the electoral votes for vice-president. If no one has over half, then the Senate chooses the vice-president. The Senate chooses from the two people with the most electoral votes on the list. In order for the Senate to vote on this, at least two-thirds of all the senators must be present. The winner needs more than half the votes of all the senators.

According to the Constitution, if a person cannot run for president, that person cannot run for vice-president. They both must have the same qualifications.

Amendment 13 (1865)
Section 1. Slavery is not allowed in the United States. It is not allowed in any land ruled by the United States. Forced labor, that is, being forced to work, is not allowed except as a legal punishment for doing a crime.

Section 2. Congress has the power to make laws that will make this amendment work.

Amendment 14 (1868)
Section 1. Citizens are all people who are born in the United States. Citizens are also persons who are naturalized, that is, legally made into citizens. All citizens are under

shall make or enforce any law which shall abridge the privileges or immunities of citizens of the United States; nor shall any State deprive any person of life, liberty, or property, without due process of law; nor deny to any person within its jurisdiction the equal protection of the laws.

the rule of the United States government. They are citizens of both the United States and the state in which they live. No state can make or enforce a law that keeps people from getting their rights as United States citizens.

No state can take anyone's life, liberty, or property without the due process of law. [Note: The courts decide the ways that this protects rights. The 5th Amendment told the federal government to follow due process of law.] No state can keep a person from getting equal treatment from its laws.

Section 2—Representatives shall be apportioned among the several States according to their respective numbers, counting the whole number of persons in each State, ~~excluding Indians not taxed.~~ But when the right to vote at any election for the choice of electors for President and Vice President of the United States, Representatives in Congress, the Executive and Judicial officers of a State, or the members of the Legislature thereof, is denied to any of the ~~male~~ inhabitants of such State, ~~being twenty-one years of age,~~ and citizens of the United States, or in any way abridged, except for participation in rebellion, or other crime, the basis of representation therein shall be reduced in the proportion which the number of such ~~male~~ citizens shall bear to the whole number of ~~male~~ citizens ~~twenty-one years of age~~ in such State.

Section 2. Representatives in Congress are given to states according to the number of people states have. All people shall be counted except untaxed Indians. [Note: This does away with the counting of a slave as three-fifths of a person.] A state shall lose representatives according to the number of people it keeps from voting. [Note: This part of Section 2 was supposed to get former slave states to allow African-American men to vote.] Voters must be male citizens who are 21 or over. They must not have done any crimes that would keep them from voting. [Note: The parts of this section about nontaxed Native Americans and limiting rights to males and those 21 or over are no longer in effect.]

Section 3—No person shall be a Senator or Representative in Congress, or elector of President and Vice President, or hold any office, civil or military, under the United States, or under any State, who, having previously taken an oath, as a member of Congress, or as an officer of the United States, or as a member of any State legislature, or as an executive or judicial officer of any State, to support the Constitution of the United States, shall have engaged in insurrection or rebellion against the same, or given aid or comfort to the enemies thereof. But Congress may by a vote of two-thirds of each House, remove such disability.

Section 3. No person shall hold government office who once took the oath of office and then became a Confederate leader. But Congress could remove this punishment by a two-thirds vote of both houses.

Section 4—The validity of the public debt of the United States, authorized by law, including debts incurred for payment of pensions and bounties for services in suppressing insurrection or rebellion, shall not be questioned. But neither the United States nor any State shall assume or pay any debt or obligation incurred in aid of insurrection or rebellion against the United States, or any claim for the loss or emancipation of any slave; but all such debts, obligations and claims shall be held illegal and void.

Section 4. The debts of the United States in ending the rebellion (the Civil War) are legal. These debts will be paid. The United States will not pay debts that the Southern states made in fighting against the U.S. government. None of the states is allowed to pay these debts either. No payment can be made for slaves who have been set free.

Section 5—The Congress shall have the power to enforce, by appropriate legislation, the provisions of this article.

Section 5. Congress shall have power to make laws that will make this amendment work.

Article XV
Section 1—The right of citizens of the United States to vote shall not be denied or abridged by the United States or by any State on account of race, color, or previous condition of servitude.

Amendment 15 (1870)
Section 1. Neither the United States nor any state government may keep citizens from voting because of their race or their color or because they were once slaves.

Section 2—The Congress shall have power to enforce this article by appropriate legislation.

Section 2. Congress has the power to make laws that will make this amendment work.

Article XVI
The Congress shall have power to lay and collect taxes on incomes, from whatever source derived, without apportionment among the several States, and without regard to any census or enumeration.

Amendment 16 (1913)
Congress has the power to tax and to collect taxes from incomes. It doesn't matter how a person may get the income. Congress does not have to follow the old rules of getting a certain amount of these taxes from each state based on population.

Article
The Senate of the United States shall be composed of two Senators from each State, elected by the people thereof, for six years; and each Senator shall have one vote. The electors in each State shall have the qualifications requisite for electors of the most numerous branch of the State legislatures.

Amendment 17 (1913)
The Senate is made up of two senators from each state. The senators are elected by the people of their state. They are elected for six-year terms. Each senator has one vote. People who can vote for members of the larger house in their state legislature can also vote for senators. [Note: This is the same rule that is used to decide who can vote for members of the House of Representatives. This means that if people can vote for members of one house of Congress they can vote for members of the other house of Congress.]

When vacancies happen in the representation of any State in the Senate, the executive authority of such State shall issue writs of election to fill such vacancies: *Provided,* That the legislature of any State may empower the executive thereof to make temporary appointments until the people fill the vacancies by election as the legislature may direct.

This amendment shall not be so construed as to affect the election or term of any Senator chosen before it becomes valid as part of the Constitution.

Article
Section 1—After one year from the ratification of this article the manufacture, sale, or transportation of intoxicating liquors within, the importation thereof into, or the exportation thereof from the United States and all territory subject to the jurisdiction thereof for beverage purposes is hereby prohibited.

Section 2—The Congress and the several States shall have concurrent power to enforce this article by appropriate legislation.

Section 3—This article shall be inoperative unless it shall have been ratified as an amendment to the Constitution by the legislatures of the several States, as provided in the Constitution, within seven years from the date of the submission hereof to the States by the Congress.

Article
The right of citizens of the United States to vote shall not be denied or abridged by the United States or by any State on account of sex.

Congress shall have power to enforce this article by appropriate legislation.

Article
*Section 1—The terms of the President and Vice President shall end at noon on the 20th day of January, and the terms of Senators and Representatives at noon on the 3d day of

A vacancy may happen among a state's U.S. senators. Then the governor of that state calls for a new election. The state legislature may allow the governor to appoint someone as acting senator until the election takes place. The legislature says how and when the election shall be held.

This amendment did not affect the election or term of office of any senator chosen before the amendment became a part of the Constitution.

Amendment 18 (1919)
Section 1. One year after the amendment was ratified, the following rules were to go into effect. It was forbidden to make, sell, or transport intoxicating beverages within the United States. It was forbidden to bring them into the United States or into any land it controlled. It was forbidden to send them out of the United States or out of any land it controlled.

Section 2. Congress and the states could pass laws to enforce this prohibition.

Section 3. This article was not to become part of the Constitution unless it was made into an amendment within seven years. [Note: This amendment was repealed in 1933 by the 21st Amendment.]

Amendment 19 (1920)
Section 1. The United States or any state government cannot keep citizens from voting because of their sex.

Section 2. Congress has the power to make laws that will make this amendment work.

Amendment 20 (1933)
Section 1. The old president and the old vice-president leave office at noon on January 20. The new president and vice-president take office at that time. Old members

January, of the years in which such terms would have ended if this article had not been ratified; and the terms of their successors shall then begin.

Section 2—The Congress shall assemble at least once in every year, and such meeting shall begin at noon on the 3d day of January, unless they shall by law appoint a different day.

Section 3—If, at the time fixed for the beginning of the term of the President, the President elect shall have died, the Vice President elect shall become President. If a President shall not have been chosen before the time fixed for the beginning of his term, or if the President elect shall have failed to qualify, then the Vice President elect shall act as President until a President shall have qualified; and the Congress may by law provide for the case wherein neither a President elect nor a Vice President elect shall have qualified, declaring who shall then act as President, or the manner in which one who is to act shall be selected, and such person shall act accordingly until a President or Vice President shall have qualified.

Section 4—The Congress may by law provide for the case of the death of any of the persons from whom the House of Representatives may choose a President whenever the right of choice shall have devolved upon them, and for the case of the death of any of the persons from whom the Senate may choose a Vice President whenever the right of choice shall have devolved upon them.

Section 5—Sections 1 and 2 shall take effect on the 15th day of October following the ratification of this article.

Section 6—This article shall be inoperative unless it shall have been ratified as an amendment to the Constitution by the legislatures of three-fourths of the several States within seven years from the date of its submission.

---

of Congress leave office at noon on January 3. New members of Congress take office at that time.

Section 2. Congress must meet at least once a year. This will be on January 3 unless Congress passes a law for another meeting time. [Note: This changed Article 1, Section 4, clause 2.]

Section 3. If the president-elect dies before taking office, the vice-president-elect becomes president. If there is no qualified president-elect by the time his or her term is supposed to start, the vice-president-elect becomes acting president. Congress may pass a law for cases when there is no qualified vice-president-elect either. In such a case, the law Congress passes can allow Congress to choose someone to be acting president. This law of Congress can set up some other way to choose an acting president until a president or vice president qualifies.

Section 4. If Congress has to decide who is to be president or vice-president and meanwhile one of the candidates dies, Congress will say what is to be done. [Note: Remember the rules of the 12th Amendment. If no candidate for president gets a majority of electoral votes, the House picks the president from the top three. If no vice-president gets a majority of electoral votes, the Senate picks from the top two. This section of the 20th Amendment tells what happens if one of these candidates dies.]

Section 5. Sections 1 and 2 of this amendment start on October 15, following approval of this amendment.

Section 6. This amendment had to be ratified within seven years from when it was sent to the states.

Article

Section 1—The eighteenth article of amendment to the Constitution of the United States is hereby repealed.

Section 2—The transportation or importation into any State, Territory, or possession of the United States for delivery or use therein of intoxicating liquors, in violation of the laws thereof, is hereby prohibited.

Section 3—This article shall be inoperative unless it shall have been ratified as an amendment to the Constitution by conventions in the several States, as provided in the Constitution, within seven years from the date of the submission hereof to the States by the Congress.

Article

Section 1—No person shall be elected to the office of the President more than twice, and no person who has held the office of President, or acted as President, for more than two years of a term to which some other person was elected President shall be elected to the office of the President more than once. But this Article shall not apply to any person holding the office of President when this Article was proposed by the Congress, and shall not prevent any person who may be holding the office of President, or acting as President, during the term within which this Article becomes operative from holding the office of President or acting as President during the remainder of such term.

Section 2—This article shall be inoperative unless it shall have been ratified as an amendment to the Constitution by the legislatures of three-fourths of the several States within seven years from the date of its submission to the States by the Congress.

Article

Section 1—The District constituting the seat of Government of the United States shall appoint in such manner as the Congress may direct:

A number of electors of President and Vice President equal to the whole number of

Amendment 21 (1933)
Section 1. The 18th Amendment of the Constitution is now repealed. (Prohibition is no longer a federal law.)

Section 2. Where it is forbidden to do so, it is illegal to bring intoxicating liquor into any state, territory, or land owned by the United States.

Section 3. This rule does not become an amendment of the Constitution unless state meetings vote for it. They must do so within seven years. These meetings must follow the rules for passing amendments that are written in the Constitution.

Amendment 22 (1951)
Section 1. Nobody may be elected to the office of president more than twice. Either holding the office or acting as president for more than two years counts as one term of office. This amendment did not apply to the person who was president when it was suggested or ratified.

Section 2. This amendment had to be ratified within seven years from when it was sent to the states.

Amendment 23 (1961)
Section 1. The District of Columbia is to choose electors for president and vice-president. The number of electors is to be the same as if it were a state. However, it may not have more electors than the state with the least population.

Senators and Representatives in Congress to which the District would be entitled if it were a State, but in no event more than the least populous State; they shall be in addition to those appointed by the States, but they shall be considered, for the purposes of the election of President and Vice President, to be electors appointed by a State; and they shall meet in the District and perform such duties as provided by the twelfth article of amendment.

Section 2—The Congress shall have power to enforce this article by appropriate legislation.

Section 2. Congress has the power to make laws in order to make this amendment work.

Article
Section 1—The right of citizens of the United States to vote in any primary or other election for President or Vice President, for electors for President or Vice President, or for Senator or Representative in Congress, shall not be denied or abridged by the United States or any State by reason of failure to pay any poll tax or other tax.

Amendment 24 (1964)
Section 1. Every citizen of the United States has the right to vote. They can vote in any primary election. They can vote in any election for president or vice-president. They may vote for electors for president or vice-president. They may vote for senators or representatives in Congress. Neither the United States government nor any state government can keep citizens from using their voting rights because they have not paid a poll tax or other tax.

Section 2—The Congress shall have power to enforce this article by appropriate legislation.

Section 2. Congress has the power to make any laws that are needed to make this amendment work.

Article
Section 1—In case of the removal of the President from office or of his death or resignation, the Vice President shall become President.

Amendment 25 (1967)
Section 1. In case the president is removed from office, dies, or resigns, the vice-president becomes president.

Section 2—Whenever there is a vacancy in the office of the Vice President, the President shall nominate a Vice President who shall take office upon confirmation by a majority vote of both Houses of Congress.

Section 2. Two steps are to be taken if for some reason there is no vice-president. First, the president names the person he or she wishes to be vice-president. Second, a majority, that is, more than half of both houses of Congress, must vote in favor of that person's becoming vice-president. Then that person becomes vice-president.

Section 3—Whenever the President transmits to the President pro tempore of the Senate and the Speaker of the House of Representatives his written declaration that he is unable to

Section 3. If the president cannot work any longer, he or she must say this in writing two times. First, the president must write a note to the leader (president pro tempore)

discharge the powers and duties of his office, and until he transmits to them a written declaration to the contrary, such powers and duties shall be discharged by the Vice President as Acting President.

Section 4—Whenever the Vice President and a majority of either the principal officers of the executive departments or of such other body as Congress may by law provide, transmit to the President pro tempore of the Senate and the Speaker of the House of Representatives their written declaration that the President is unable to discharge the powers and duties of his office, the Vice President shall immediately assume the powers and duties of the office as Acting President.

Thereafter, when the President transmits to the President pro tempore of the Senate and the Speaker of the House of Representatives his written declaration that no inability exists, he shall resume the powers and duties of his office unless the Vice President and a majority of either the principal officers of the executive department or of such other body as Congress may by law provide, transmit within four days to the President pro tempore of the Senate and the Speaker of the House of Representatives their written declaration that the President is unable to discharge the powers and duties of his office. Thereupon Congress shall decide the issue, assembling within forty-eight hours for that purpose if not in session. If the Congress, within twenty-one days after receipt of the latter written declaration, or, if Congress is not in session, within twenty-one days after Congress is required to assemble, determines by two-thirds vote of both Houses that the President is unable to discharge the powers and duties of his office, the Vice President shall continue to discharge the same as Acting President; otherwise, the President shall resume the powers and duties of his office.

of the Senate. Second, the president must also write to the Speaker of the House of Representatives. After these letters are written, the vice-president becomes acting president. The acting president then has the full powers of the president. If the president becomes well again, he or she can regain the office. To do so, the president again writes to these leaders of Congress.

Section 4. The vice-president may decide that the president is too ill to do the job. However, a majority of the president's cabinet or another group of people chosen by Congress must agree. They must then give their decision in writing to both the leader (president pro tempore) of the Senate and the Speaker of the House. The vice-president then becomes the acting president.

After getting better, the president may wish to go back to work. Then the president must send a written statement to both the leader (president pro tempore) of the Senate and the Speaker of the House. The president then regains his or her powers as president. But the vice-president and a majority of the president's cabinet or the body chosen by Congress may disagree with the president. It they do, they must say so in writing within four days to the leader (president pro tempore) of the Senate and the Speaker of the House. Congress must meet within 48 hours. Congress has 21 days to decide what to do. If at least two-thirds of the House and two-thirds of the Senate vote that the president is unable to work, then the vice-president remains as acting president. Otherwise, the president returns to office.

Article

Section 1—The right of citizens of the United States, who are eighteen years of age or older, to vote shall not be denied or abridged by the United States or by any State on account of age.

Section 2—The Congress shall have power to enforce this article by appropriate legislation.

Amendment 26 (1971)

Section 1. Eighteen-year-old citizens of the United States have the right to vote. The United States and the state governments cannot stop them from voting because of their age.

Section 2. Congress has the power to pass laws that will make this amendment work.

INDEX OF CASES

Author's Acknowledgments

I would like to thank Fred Anderson of the University of Colorado, a leading expert on the military during the colonial era, for his close reading of the manuscript. I would also like to thank Adriane Ruggiero for her fine editing, as well as Richard G. Gallin for his cheerful support. Furthermore, I would like to express my appreciation to the Calvin Coolidge Library at Castleton State College in Vermont.

Burnham Holmes's previous books for young adults have ranged in topics from what it's like to go through army basic training to what it's like to be a medical student in a hospital, from the world's first baseball game to the world's first Seeing Eye dog, from the mystery of an airplane crash to the mystery surrounding Nefertiti's life and death. He also wrote *The Fifth Amendment* for *The American Heritage History of the Bill of Rights*.

Burnham Holmes teaches writing at the School of Visual Arts in New York City and at the Community College of Vermont at Middlebury. Burnham and Vicki and their son, Ken, split their time between living in New York City and near a lake in Vermont.

Warren E. Burger was Chief Justice of the United States from 1969 to 1986. Since 1985 he has served as chairman of the Commission on the Bicentennial of the United States Constitution. He is also chancellor of the College of William and Mary, Williamsburg, Virginia; chancellor emeritus of the Smithsonian Institution; and a life trustee of the National Geographic Society. Prior to his appointment to the Supreme Court, Chief Justice Burger was Assistant Attorney General of the United States (Civil Division) and judge of the United States Court of Appeals, District of Columbia Circuit.

Philip A. Klinkner graduated from Lake Forest College in 1985 and is now finishing his Ph.D. in political science at Yale University. He is currently a Governmental Studies Fellow at the Brookings Institution in Washington, D.C. Klinkner is the author of *The First Amendment* and *The Ninth Amendment* in *The American Heritage History of the Bill of Rights*.